Flourishing
for Sports

Flourishing for Sports

Well-being of a Sportsman
from Perspectives
of Positive Psychology

Crystal Wu

PARTRIDGE

A Penguin Random House Company

To order additional copies of this book, contact
Toll Free 800 101 2657 (Singapore)
Toll Free 1 800 81 7340 (Malaysia)
orders.singapore@partridgepublishing.com

www.partridgepublishing.com/singapore

CONTENTS

PREFACE

This book is about flourishing – the latest concept about psychological well-being in the field of positive psychology. Why choose sports as the main theme? In addition to being a psychologist, I am also an enthusiastic fan of sports. It is as simple as that. I am a believer of the strength of positive psychology, which emphasises cultivating positivity in people to enhance overall well-being of life. Sports, being so popular and inspiring, are the perfect subject for conveying my understandings on well-being to readers.

The inspiration behind this book may sound a bit crazy. Some athletes inspired me so much that I felt compelled to tell others. Initially, it was just bits and pieces of positive stories. Later, when I put things together, it turned out to be quite a coherent work that linked sports and positive psychology. Unlike books about sports psychology, which usually focus on achieving sporting success and excellence, this book emphasises how athletes can draw on their own strengths to become flourished whole persons. It discusses psychology that affects both the sporting career and the normal life of an athlete. I am sharing stories of a role model, for I believe that learning from a living legend will be more fruitful and fascinating. Of course, if you are a sports fan, you will find it particularly easy and interesting to follow this book. Even if you are not, you probably will find it useful as long as you are a pursuer of happiness and a quality life.

Chapters will be arranged in accordance with the five-element model for flourishing: PERMA (positive emotion, engagement, positive relationships, meaning, and accomplishment). The following will be covered in each chapter: (1) positive psychological concepts about the element, (2) the significance and relevance of such an element in sports, (3) how the role model manifests positive psychological qualities in the area, and (4) practical guidelines on building up our respective qualities to improve overall well-being.

In this book, I encourage you to look for some valuable ideas that may help you enhance your psychological well-being. My hope is that reading this book will be an initial step leading you to a life-long journey of pursuing a flourished life of your own.

CHAPTER 1
Flourishing

What is positive psychology? What is its significance? Psychology studies human mind and behaviour and seeks to understand and explain human thought, emotion, and behaviour. Psychology has long focused on understanding and curing human sufferings, weaknesses, deficits, and particularly mental illness. Psychological interventions have been widely studied and proven effective in treating people with psychiatric disorders such as depression, anxiety disorders, psychosis, and so forth. Comparatively, the brighter side of human nature has been overlooked for many years. Nevertheless, positive psychology has been an exploding area of studies in recent years, as Dr. Martin Seligman, an American psychologist and the director of the Positive Psychology Center at the University of Pennsylvania, deliberately set out a new direction and orientation for psychology: study of human strength and virtue.

The scope of positive psychology encompasses three major areas of human experience: (1) positive individual traits (genius, creativity, optimism, and so on); (2) positive emotional states (happiness, love, optimal and peak experiences, and so forth); and

(3) institutions that enable flourishing (family, work, community, culture, and so on). Positive psychology aims to provide a more complete and balanced understanding of human experience, thereby supplementing the learning of human sufferings as well as building knowledge about the well-being of human life. The mission of positive psychology is to understand the factors that promote flourishing individuals and societies and then devise pathways to enhance those factors.

I have an overall positive orientation towards life and a natural interest in understanding positive aspects of human nature. Since I was exposed to positive psychology while earning my master's degree study in clinical psychology, I have been quite immersed in the subject, as it fits very well into my own belief system. Only after I studied positive psychology more seriously could I put all relevant concepts into a better framework. My years of experience as a clinical practitioner further reinforced my interest in positive psychology, also adding some insight into how it can be applied in our daily lives.

In psychotherapy, we deal with clients' problems and distress by facilitating them to cope better with their negative emotions, to identify and change their negative thoughts, and to enhance skills like social skills, communication, and problem-solving skills. It is quite effective for reducing their distresses and promoting their recoveries. From research and my clinical experience, I've learned that integration of positive psychology into the intervention – that is, talking about personal strengths, resilience, gratitude, happiness, and so on – can go beyond healing and add value in setting positive life orientations for our clients.

Another predominant enthusiasm of mine is sports. I have long been a lover of sports, both as a player and more so as an audience. I have practised Chinese martial arts for over twenty years. Tennis is one of my favourite sports now. I started to play tennis more seriously after Roger Federer charmed me seven or eight years ago. I enjoy hiking, running, and playing different kinds of ball games. As a fan, I follow tennis tournaments most closely. Soccer is also my priority. Snooker and golf are my casual choices. During World Cups, I cheer loud for my favourite soccer teams, and some of my favourite soccer idols are Roberto Baggio, Zinedine Zidane, and Lionel Messi. I could watch the Olympic games all day, and I'd become upset if I missed some important ones.

The two paths of my enthusiasm crossed when inspiration arose about linking positive psychology and sports together. Sports are generally positive and healthy. They help build our physical and psychological strengths. Positive psychological qualities, on the other hand, help athletes prosper in their careers and personal lives.

Psychological well-being

Definition of psychological well-being has changed over time. Before the prospering of positive psychology, psychological well-being was defined with mostly a medical approach, thus meaning largely an absence of a significant psychiatric illness or psychological problem. Later the definition extended to incorporate one's level of functioning and happiness. Happiness, as a combination of positive emotion and life satisfaction, has long been regarded as an ultimate pursuit of human beings. People have a natural inner drive to seek happiness.

Concepts of happiness have been widely studied in the field of psychology. Outside academies, many people have shared their perspectives about happiness and more so on how to pursue happiness. Books, journals, and seminars on this topic are abundant. Dr. Seligman put happiness into a better and clearer framework in his book *Authentic Happiness: Using the new positive psychology to realise your potential for lasing fulfillment*[1]. According to Dr. Seligman, happiness can be pursued through three pathways: (1) experiencing positive emotions about the past, present, and future; (2) obtaining gratification from exercising people's character strengths; and (3) using strengths in the service of something larger than self to obtain meaning.

In Dr. Seligman's latest book, *Flourish: A Visionary New Understanding of Happiness and Well-Being*[2], he advanced his theory of authentic happiness to well-being theory. He re-examined the construct of psychological well-being. He proposed that any element of well-being must possess three properties: (1) it contributes to well-being, (2) many people pursue it for its own sake, not merely to get any of the other elements, and (3) it is defined and measured independently of the other elements. Under such criteria, Dr. Seligman derived five constituting elements for well-being: positive emotion, engagement, positive relationships, meaning, and accomplishment. The mnemonic for the well-being theory is *PERMA*. Flourishing, as the goal of positive psychology, means fulfilment in an individual's PERMA. The framework of this book will be largely based on this model.

Flourishing in sports

Any person in any profession can become flourished. I chose to investigate flourishing in sports because of the wide public interest and my own enthusiasm in them. In addition, sports are unique in the sense that exercise involved in sports produces endorphins, a brain chemical that can generate a feeling of well-being.

How is PERMA exhibited in the world of sports? Positive emotions experienced in sports can be quite overwhelming. So often, we are moved by an athlete's raw expression of emotions – for example, tears of joy after winning. At the professional level, many athletes simply enjoy what they have been doing despite the usual stress, anxiety, and disappointments involved during their pursuits of success. Sources of positive emotions are abundant: joy of winning, gratification of achieving goals, excitement during competition, enthusiasm in the sport itself, appreciation of sheer excellence of others, gratefulness for doing something they love for a living … The list goes on. Even at a recreational level, with the right mindsets, we can experience similar positive emotions.

Sports are highly engaging activities, as they usually require coordination among our different senses, muscles, and body parts. They demand us to devote our full attention to here and now. When we are playing the sports we love, it feels as if time flies.

Relationships play a significant role in team sports. Collaboration and mutual support in team sports can have a positive effect on an individual's performance and feelings. Even in individual sports, in order to feel good, athletes have to cultivate positive relationships with their own support teams, including coaches, physiologists, and managers, in addition to other closely related parties such as other athletes, sports journalists, fans, and so forth.

For professional athletes, sports are their careers. Career, in general, means a lot to any person. It is an important source for earning income, making accomplishments, building social networks, and enhancing self-esteem. Sports have attracted attention from all over the word. Therefore, as public figures, athletes often assume meaningful roles in inspiring others. Top athletes see themselves as leaders in promoting their respective sports. Celebrities in the sports world are often involved in charity work, hopefully making good use of publicity to help less fortunate populations around the globe.

Accomplishments in sports can be explicitly measured, for example, by how many trophies have been won, how many awards have been granted, what ranking has been achieved, and what records have been set. At the professional level, sports are very goal-driven. Athletes set their own goals and carefully plan their training accordingly. Some of them have very ambitious goals. Some of them take on a more gradual approach. In any case, they recognise that sense of accomplishment is a strong motivational factor for them to keep working. The gratification of accomplishing goals adds much more to one's well-being than monetary rewards.

Flourished role model

When we were little kids, we all needed role models to look up to. Even as grown-ups, the need is still there, except that we make more conscious choices in selecting those we wish to model. I made a well-considered decision to pick Roger Federer, a respectable tennis player, as a role model for flourishing. I will share stories of him in this book to hopefully make my presentations more coherent and lively as well as make your learning about well-being more interesting. You may or may not know much about him. Don't worry. You will get to know him a little bit more and be impressed by how well he has carried himself as an honourable person.

Roger Federer, an ATP (Association of Tennis Professionals) tennis player, was voted the second most respected person in the world, after former South African president Nelson Mandela, in a survey conducted by the Reputation Institute in 2011. The survey involved over fifty thousand people from twenty-five countries; the respondents expressed their attitudes towards fifty-four public figures from politics, business, sports, and culture. Roger Federer not only receives widespread admiration for his legendary accomplishments in tennis but is also a publicly respected person with a great personality.

Many people have tried to outline the personality of this global celebrity. Paul E. Farrow, a tennis professional, in an article he wrote for *Tennis Week* in 2006[3], described Federer in this way: 'The demeanor, integrity, self-confidence and overall manner of Federer set him apart from many of his peers. He is tough, gritty and hard-nosed on the inside, yet gentle, compassionate, funny, sincere and soft spoken on the outside.' I see him as a person with clearly identifiable character strengths. From what I have seen, he is a happy and positive person who enjoys what he has been doing. He embraces his life. He is a natural believer of the power of positivity.

Here is some information about Federer and his major achievements:

Personal profile:

Name:	Roger Federer
Birthdate:	8 August 1981
Birthplace:	Basel, Switzerland
Languages:	Swiss German, German, English, and French
Marital status:	Married to Miroslava Vavrinec (Mirka) in 2009

Children:	Twin daughters born in 2009; twin sons born in 2014
Turned professional:	1998

Tennis accomplishments (as of June 2014):
Federer's achievements and records in tennis are numerous. Here are the most significant ones:

- Won a record seventeen Grand Slam titles, breaking the previous all-time male record of fourteen, held by Pete Sampras
- Won a total of seventy-nine single titles in his career
- Was ranked number one for a record 302 weeks
- Was ranked number one for a record 237 consecutive weeks, surpassing the previous record of 160 consecutive weeks, held by Jimmy Connors
- Won Wimbledon seven times, a record he shares with Pete Sampras
- Won ATP Tour Finals/Masters Cups a record six times
- Reached a record twenty-three consecutive Grand Slam semi-finals (2004 Wimbledon – 2010 Australian Open), breaking the previous male record of ten consecutive Grand Slam semi-finals, shared by Ivan Lendl and Rod Laver

Awards and honours:
Federer received dozens of awards and honours. He was honoured for his tennis success, sportsmanship, humanity, and popularity. Here are some significant ones:

- Laureus World Sportsman of the Year: a record four consecutive years (2005–2008)

- International Tennis Federation (ITF) World Champion: five times (2004–2007, 2009)
- Swiss Athlete of the Year: five times (2003–2007, 2012)
- Stefan Edberg Sportsmanship Award: a record nine times (2004–2009, 2011-2013)
- Prix Orange for fair play: five times (2005–2009)
- ATP Fans' Favourite Award: a record eleven consecutive years (2003–2013)
- UNICEF Goodwill Ambassador: in 2006
- Arthur Ashe Humanitarian of the Year: two times (2006, 2013)

CHAPTER 2
Positive Emotions (P)

Experiencing positive emotions is significant for development of psychological well- being. A well-established 'broaden and build' model of positive emotions, proposed by Dr. Barbara Fredrickson, the Kenan distinguished professor of psychology and principal investigator of the Positive Emotions and Psychophysiology Lab at the University of North Carolina, formulates a framework in explaining underlying mechanisms of how positive emotions help fulfil the psychological needs of human beings. The model suggests that positive emotions broaden people's momentary thought-action repertoires and build their enduring personal resources, ranging from physical and intellectual resources to social and psychological resources.

Positive emotions broaden our attention, enable us to have more creative and flexible ideas, and help fuel our psychological resiliency. Positive emotions can also trigger an upward spiral effect. In other words, the emotions drive us into actions that further elicit more emotions that are positive. The above establishes the role of positive emotions in enhancing the psychological well-being of individuals.

There are three basic dimensions of positive emotions: joviality, meaning happiness, joy, and enthusiasm; assurance, meaning confidence and bravery; and attentiveness, meaning determination and concentration. There are certain basic positive emotions which can be coupled in various ways to constitute more emotions that are complex and create more subtle variations. Happiness, enjoyment, interest, and anticipation are considered basic positive emotions; happiness has been the most widely explored and is identified as the root of subjective well-being. What is happiness? Happiness is considered more than just a transient positive emotional state. It is an overall sense of emotional well-being and satisfaction with life. It involves a resulting balance of all positive and negative emotional experiences over a certain period.

Is a person's enduring level of happiness inherited or changeable upon experiences? The answer to this question has important implications on whether happiness can be pursued or not. According to a set point theory that is commonly cited in positive psychology, most people have their own average levels of happiness, which they go back to after adjusting to temporary highs and lows in emotionality. While there is the matter of heritability in determining the level of happiness, environmental factors also play a significant role. Therefore, one can influence her level of well-being by engaging or creating environments that are conductive to feelings of happiness. Dr. Seligman's happiness formula[1] proposed that an enduring level of happiness is derived from combining effects of a person's happiness set range, circumstances of a person's life, and factors under a person's voluntary control.

$$H = S + C + V$$

H is enduring level of happiness, S is set range, C is the circumstances of life, and V represents factors under voluntary control.

Similar to the set point theory, set range in the formula is the biologically predetermined range of emotionality. Life circumstances such as education, family, social interactions, and religion are contributing factors for adjusting the durable happiness level. Individuals can also voluntarily work on personal attributes, such as gratitude, forgiving, and optimism, to uplift the enduring level of happiness. I think this theory should give us some hope and drive to pursue our own happiness.

Remember that the happiness we talk about here is more than a sense of pleasure in the present moment. A happy life involves feeling positive about the past, the present, and the future. For example, we may feel grateful and satisfied for what we have attained in the past, be positively immersed in the moments right now, and be hopeful and optimistic about our futures.

Positive emotions in sports

Professional sports are competitive, and the environment can be rather stressful. In pursuit of a successful career in sports, there is never a shortage of experiences to elicit an athlete's negative feelings, whether anxiety about matches, frustration about failures, inward anger due to mistakes made by oneself, outward rage due to someone's violation of fairness in competition, or regret for making wrong decisions.

The career of a professional athlete usually starts early and is relatively short. Therefore, early cultivation of a positive mindset is particularly important because there is only a short time span for an athlete to mature enough to deal with the psychological hurdles encountered. In the history of sports, many athletes have failed to bring their talent into full play because they were overwhelmed by negative emotions that impaired their capacities to exert their potentials.

There is an obvious prerequisite for experiencing happiness: acknowledging the value of happiness. Happy people want to be happy, and they place happiness at the top of their priority lists. They also value the happiness of the people they love. There is a myth that says, 'The surest way to lose happiness is to pursue it directly.' But I think it is true only when one becomes too obsessed with pursuing happiness. Happy people do think about and seek the best ways to pursue happiness.

In many interviews, Federer could not emphasise enough that he was a happy person. He once even said that he sometimes felt he was one of the happiest persons in the world. No doubt his success has brought him abundant joy and gratification, but it cannot be the sole contributing factor to his happiness. Accomplishment does not guarantee happiness, as it usually comes with stress, expectations, and responsibilities.

Look at the case of Andre Agassi. He was a great tennis champion with so much charisma. Yet even at his peak, we could hardly feel that he was immersed in happiness. He appeared to feel uneasy about his status and did not really enjoy what he was doing. He was almost avoidant of the responsibilities that went with his success. He became a more settled and happier man only after he started a family with his lovely wife, Steffi Graf, raising their children. His growing role later in the charity business also added to his life satisfaction.

On the other hand, happiness has always been in the heart of Roger Federer. A reporter for the *Miami Herald* asked Federer a simple question in 2006: 'The best feeling you've ever known?'

Federer simply answered, 'Happiness.' On Federer's home page, there is an 'Ask Roger' page, where Federer answers questions posted by fans. This was one of the questions asked of him: 'What do you think is your greatest quality?' Federer again gave a straightforward answer: 'I'm a very happy person.'

In the tennis world, people undoubtedly care more about players' accomplishments than happiness. Whether or not a player plays happily is not much of a concern. Federer does demonstrate well how a player can pursue happiness by achieving goals and can accomplish more by playing happily. Federer is aware that having a happy life helps his tennis. 'I think I've handled many things the right way, including the media, my personal life ... I always kept things happy. I think that's key to a long career,' Federer said in the press conference after winning his fifteenth Grand Slam at Wimbledon. Accomplishments bring happiness only when people truly appreciate their achievements and truly value happiness.

Assuming you do want to play your sport(s) happily, in the following paragraphs, I will help you to recognise the positive emotions you may experience in doing sports.

Joviality

Joy of winning: Almost all sports are competitive win-lose games. Whether sports are punch and counterpunch games (such as tennis, badminton, and boxing) or more self-focused performing games (such as golf and gymnastics), there are still winners and losers. Therefore, the joy of winning and the frustration of losing are two opposite ends of feelings about the results. A positive psychological approach prefers winning to feel more joy rather than winning to avoid frustration.

In a 2007 Nike commercial featuring both Roger Federer and Tiger Woods, an interesting exchange towards the end had Federer saying, 'I love winning,' contrasted by Woods saying, 'I hate losing.' That was somewhat of an advertising gimmick. However, it did present different approaches in competitive sports: whether athletes are motivated by their longings for positive feelings, are repulsed by negative feelings, or both. Federer believed he was the 'love winning' type rather than the 'hate losing' type. He talked about his lack of demons in his love of the game in an interview by the *Sunday Times* in 2009. He said, 'Well, I'm a positive person, a very positive thinker. That's why I like the more positive approach of "I love winning", because to hate losing, to me, is a bit negative.'[4]

Federer demonstrated well how an athlete can obtain the greatest pleasure by absorbing themselves in the joy and pride of winning. Two weeks after winning his first French Open title, which had eluded him for so long, Reuters asked Federer if the win was more of a relief or more of a joyous occasion. He answered firmly, 'It was more of a high joy than relief.' He explained further: 'I don't like seeing victories as release. Because it's not the way it's supposed to be. Of course, it was an enormous amount of pressure. It's a relief at some stage, but the joy is much, much bigger.'

To me, watching athletes shedding tears of joy is very moving. It feels as if I am sharing the victorious moment with joy. Such raw expressions of positive emotions can be quite powerful. Many times, I have seen audiences feel so touched that their eyes get moist when they clap and cheer. Federer has probably cried in public more than any other champion. He shed joyful tears when he won his first Grand Slam title (Wimbledon, 2003). Such an outburst of positive emotions stirred up tears from his Swiss fans in the stadium. Feeling emotional with Rod Laver, a tennis legend, presenting the trophy to him at the 2006 Australian Open, Federer gave his victory speech mostly in tears and finished it with a touching hug with Laver. When winning his first and only French Open title, Federer could not hold off his tears again in front of the ascending Swiss flag. We can probably conclude that the joy of winning means so much to him that he is never embarrassed to express it in public.

Enthusiasm: If winning were the only occasion in which we could feel positive doing sports, then sports would not be so popular across the globe. There's no doubt that the joy of winning is very rewarding, but the prospect of experiencing it should not be the sole motivator for athletes to get through their long hours of training, day in and day out. OK, let us not to be too romantic about this. Monetary reward is definitely one of the motivational factors for professional athletes to work hard. But many people, professional or recreational, play sports out of pure enthusiasm for them.

Enthusiasm is about intense feelings of enjoyment, interest, and passion about a certain thing. We can be enthusiastic about science, nature, arts, and almost anything. Such passion can be innate or cultivated, or it is usually a good combination of both. In most cases, enthusiasm results from a series of positive exploitations of our interests and abilities. In sports, enthusiasm may be more overtly displayed when the athlete is having his best times. In bad times, the focus is more on their frustrations and defeated spirits. Does it mean that enthusiasm vaporises suddenly in down times? Is winning the only way to regain the passion? I don't think so. On the contrary, I believe enthusiasm is crucial in bad times, as it makes a person more likely to be immune to overwhelming negative emotions.

Federer, who has been recognised as one of the most passionate guys the tennis tour has ever had, has probably been asked a hundred times about his level of passion towards the game. When he was asked the question during a press conference after the 2013 US Open, whereas 2013 was his worst year in terms of career achievements in the past ten years, he gave an insightful opinion about what passion really is. 'Clearly when you win everything, it's fun,' Federer said. 'That doesn't necessarily mean you love the game more. You just like winning, being on the front page, lifting trophies, doing comfortable press conferences. It's nice. But that doesn't mean you really actually love it, love it. That maybe shines through more in times when you don't play that well. For me, I knew it, winning or losing, practice court or match court, that I love it.' He sounded so convincing that you have to believe what he said.

Fun: When we first approach a type of sport, we try to find fun in doing it. People start to have fun learning the basic skills. For example, in ball games, we have fun controlling the balls to make the trajectories and motions they are supposed to score, using rackets (tennis, table tennis, badminton, squash, and so on) or our bare hands (baseball, volleyball, handball, rugby, and so forth). One of the reasons football is so popular is because it is great fun to be able to control the ball so skilfully with different parts of a body. In gymnastics, they enjoy stretching their bodies to make beautiful postures and balanced moves. After a good build-up of skills, we look for more fun by varying our games and tactics to improve our performances.

Good coaches are creative in making daily training a bit more fun to minimise aversive feelings like boredom. Many tennis players have admitted that they've tried some trick shots during their practice to have fun rather than making the shots as regular weapons. The famous trick shot in tennis is tweener, where a player hits a tennis ball between the legs. Federer perhaps is one of the most successful tennis players in executing the tweener. He's tried it even in crucial moments of the matches. Many times when successfully executing the tweener and scoring, he immediately lost his composure and laughed, even as he was playing under the heat in the biggest stadium during a slam competition. Similarly, when soccer players score with overhead kicks, in addition to showing off their brilliance, they are having fun.

Excitement: Watching a sporting event is typically exciting, especially when the occasion is big or the competition is close. Have you ever been so excited that you screamed at your TV while rooting for your favourite athlete or team? There's no doubt that athletes themselves ought to be even more excited and energised by playing the sports they love. Excitement is a very tempting feeling, even more so for energetic people with good physiques, as it helps in channelling out the inner power of a person.

Luckily, athletes can get excited in many ways. They get excited when they are playing in big occasions. For the Olympics and the World Cup, which take place only once every four years, athletes are so eager that they usually start talking about it years before the event. A good atmosphere from audiences can also stimulate the players. In tennis matches, we have seen players deliberately make gestures to call for cheers from the crowd to energise them, such as when they fall much behind in the matches. In addition, when facing challenges, we get excited, if not discouraged. Athletes with positive mindsets actually welcome challenge, whether it comes from chasing records, fierce competition, physical limitations, or aging bodies.

Self-Assurance

Self-assurance is about feeling proud, strong, confident, bold, or fearless. It is a state of positive feeling and mind. In winning situations, alongside joyfulness is a feeling of pride. Compared to joy, pride is relatively long-lived and exerts a more enduring effect on one's well-being because it helps enhance one's self-esteem. Pride boosts one's self-confidence and as a result uplifts one's performance. Athletes often mention confidence as a vital factor in determining the outcome. For example, when tennis players are on winning streaks, they often feel invincible and execute their game plans and play their best shots more decisively. When they become fearless, they become extremely hard to beat.

Positive people can feel proud of themselves even when they lose – whether it's for fighting as hard as they can with their full spirits or for bringing their performances beyond their usual levels. Whenever we have a chance, we should partake in some pride, just like accumulating savings in our banking accounts. In case of adversity, we then have enough reserve of esteem to put us through. The self-assurance we gain from doing sports not only helps us enhance performance and competitive edge in the sport itself, but it also helps us build our esteem as people, thereby strengthening determination in achieving our goals in other life areas as well.

Attentiveness

Attentiveness is a positive state of full alertness and awareness. Sports usually require us to be highly focused, with all our physical senses being oriented to make an efficient or powerful motion. Regular participation in an activity that demands high concentration can train us to perceive and to feel the events around us better. In sports, concentration is performance enhancing in many ways. When we concentrate, our thoughts and senses are totally on the task, thereby automatically screening out unnecessary distractions, including our own negative thoughts. Concentration improves our anticipation too, which is regarded as one of the major skills in sports. Concentration also arouses our feeling of determination and vice versa.

In psychology, it is a basic understanding that emotion, whether negative or positive, is not just a direct product of a situation but a result of how people perceive the situation. Cognitive appraisal plays a significant role in our everyday emotions. A positive orientation in one's mindset sets a person up for experiencing positive emotions. In sports, there is a classical situation that even experiencing the joy of winning is not as simple as it appears to be. There has been some evidence supporting that an athlete winning a bronze medal may actually be happier than the one winning the silver medal. An athlete who wins a silver medal may perceive the situation as losing a gold medal rather than winning the silver, and thus feelings of disappointment can substantially dampen feelings of joy. I followed all kinds of sports during the Olympics. I saw enough disappointing and tearful faces of athletes who finished second in their respective competitions.

Roger Federer, who was considered to have his best and last chance to chase the missing Olympic gold medal on his resume, was defeated in the final at the London Olympics in 2012. What did we get from him? 'I felt like I won my silver; I didn't lose it. So I feel very, very happy.' His positive attitude truly impressed me. Federer does not play with inner demons as John McEnroe and Andre Agassi possibly did. Agassi openly admitted in his autobiography that he hated tennis for most of his career. Federer, on the other hand, got absorbed in the joy of playing tennis and winning matches, which creates an upward spiral effect on his happiness as a player and as a person as well. He believes that sports can do great things. Such belief guides him to help giving underprivileged children, through his foundation, more opportunities to do sports and to experience happiness from doing sports.

Here we are going to learn more about how a positive mindset can help an athlete refrain from being tired out in such a highly pressured career.

1) *Take positives from competition:* Rivalry is an honour given to two sports players who bring out the most vigorous competition against each other in the same era. In soccer, we currently have Lionel Messi versus Christiano Ronaldo, even though they are playing a team sport. In tennis, since the competition is more head-on, history has dozens of well-known rivalries: Chris Evert versus Martina Navratilova, Steffi Graf versus Monica Seles, Bjorn Borg versus John McEnroe, Stefan Edberg versus Boris Becker, Andre Agassi versus Pete Sampras, and Roger Federer versus Rafael Nadal.

Rivalry in sports surely is exciting for fans, who simply enjoy the sparkle made by it, and for the media, who create fascinating stories about it. Nevertheless, there is a downside to it. Rivalry can turn out to be a tiring burden for a player if the athlete starts to see the rival as an enemy. Negative emotions such as anxiety, frustration, anger, or even hatred may take charge. It can get even worse when the media becomes fond of making negative stories about the rivalry. The worst we have seen are verbal wars and even unsportsmanlike acts during or after competition. For the professional athlete, being able to take positives from rivalry is necessary for staying positive in the sport.

Not many people recognise the upside of a rivalry. Federer does. His positive approach towards his rivalry with Nadal has definitely helped improve his own game; he also established a friendship with Nadal and set a proper and harmonious tone for the sport. He explained his positive orientation towards the rivalry in an interview with the journalist of the *Sunday Times* in 2009.[4] 'I'm surprised myself by the degree to which we [referring to Nadal and himself] actually get along because we've had a very intense rivalry and you could say he has hurt my career and that I've hurt his career, but we've actually helped each other become the players we are today. And the rivalry has helped the game. It's nice that the two greatest players in tennis, or in a sport, actually get along well, because normally there is all this hate and it's so negative, and I don't like that. We've had enough controversy in recent years with athletes, and it's a welcome change.'

2) *Take positives from defeats*: The frustrations of losing can have devastating effects on one's confidence, and eventually on one's professional career, if one fails to deal with defeats in a constructive way. There is no point denying our negative feelings, for they are as natural as our positive feelings. All we need to do is to let those feelings sink in, accept them, and express them properly. We have to avoid getting ourselves stuck in defeat for too long. More proactively, we can try to reframe those defeats positively.

Positive reframing is a skill that enables us to reconsider our frame of reference and perspective in different and more positive angles. For example, there were several occasions where Federer played some tournaments with injuries and finally lost it in the semi-finals or finals. Rather than focusing on the negative of losing, he chose to see the positive of making it that far in the tournament despite injury. As far as shocking defeats, following his disappointment and outright acceptance of the defeats, he sometimes took them as unexpected breaks he could use to rest or to prepare for the next tournament.

In an interview by the *Times of India* back in 2006, Federer was asked what his biggest defeat was and how he took criticism. Federer responded easily and said, 'There was no big defeat for me. I'm very happy with all my results; moreover, I do not take a tennis match as a huge defeat. Every time I lose a match, I get to learn something, and it gives me even more experience.'[5] Federer did well in positively reframing the criticisms directed to him and making good use of the reframed positives to drive him forward during his hard times.

3) *Take positives from interacting with media:* Stars in sports are under the limelight all the time. Sports journalists closely follow the stars in matches, in press conferences, in sponsorship events, and even in their private lives, in the hopes of writing some juicy stories. Media can be quite harsh sometimes. Apart from truthful criticisms, there may be some pointing out flaws. If athletes fail to understand the role of media in the industry, they may find the media very disturbing. The media play a crucial role in promoting the industry. Popularity of the sports no doubt has direct impact on how much athletes are paid. Sustainability of the industry depends on media's effort in generating enough publicity for it. Many sports journalists are doing their jobs with integrity. They report the results, analyse the matches with expert opinion, have in-depth interviews, and write decent stories.

Federer understands the dynamics. He interacts with media more positively than most of the other players on the tennis tour. He is regarded highly by the media and is considered one of the most approachable and forthcoming champions the sport has ever had. Unlike some players who treat media responsibility as a dreadful task, Federer comprehends well the meaning of media work and wants to take as many positives out of it as possible. He shared his attitude towards the media with reporters during the 2010 Indian Wells tournament: 'I know I'm not going to be able to escape the media, and so let's be open and easy and honest with everybody. Because at the end of the day, you guys tell our story to the fans who are reading the paper TV and whatever. I just think that's important. So for me, that was always the way I looked at it. And I don't want to be miserable coming to press conferences, because I can't escape them anyway. Might as well have some fun with it and make it interesting.'

In pursuit of happiness, a momentary state of positive emotion is just like one piece of a big puzzle. Many different pieces need to be put together to paint a lovely picture. Overall, we are happy if we feel good about our past, our present, and our future. About the past, we need to be grateful by appreciating what our past experiences have contributed to our personal growth and how they have made us become who we are. Concerning the present, we taste it the most and savour positive moments as much as possible. Regarding the future, we remain optimistic and hopeful.

Gratitude

Gratitude is a sense of thankfulness in response to receiving a gift, whether the gift is tangible, non-tangible, or a moment of delight evoked by natural beauty. It is a subjective sense of appreciation for the gift of life. It is a transcendent emotion of grace. We may feel grateful for having the relationships and things we already have. We may feel grateful towards people who have helped us. We may as well be grateful for the enlightenment that certain experiences have brought us. Gratitude, as a positive personality trait, is about having an enduring sense of thankfulness across situations and over time. People with this trait tend to enjoy better interpersonal relationships and be more contented with their lives.

How is gratitude important in sports? In the sporting world, especially within the elite group, gratitude can easily be eroded over time due to a growing sense of entitlement that often comes along with success. Unfortunately, famous athletes do receive a lot of special treatment in society. In fame, arrogance can grow. One way for them to counteract that is to remain grateful to all the people who have contributed to their careers. They have to remind themselves that they can be nobody without help from many people. When they feel grateful, they tend to give back more to the industry and thereby help the overall industry flourish. Federer, as one of the most recognised global representatives of his sport, is aware of how others have contributed to his success. He thus is more than willing to express his gratitude to coaches, competitors, sports legends, fans, the officials, and the media.

Coaches: Coaches contribute to an athlete's career most directly. Coaching support ranges from skills training, strategic planning, and body recovering to diet control, personal assistance, and counselling. If an athlete does not feel thankful to his coach, the coaching relationship is in big trouble and can only be detrimental to his sports career. Although Federer has been coachless over much of his career's prime years and is not a player who depends much on coaches, he never underrates the contributions from his coaches in his personal and tennis development. He openly expressed many times his heartfelt thanks about how Peter Carter, his coach in his teens, helped him build up his repertoire of tennis skills and develop his personality strengths.

Federer had Severin Luethi, his long-time confidante from Switzerland, as his part-time coach for several years before he got Paul Annacone on board as his full-time coach in 2010. In

2010, Federer rebounded from his relatively disappointing middle season to win several titles at the end of the season, including his precious fifth World Tour Final title. Everybody rushed on to attribute Federer's regain of form to inspiring input from his new coach. Of course, Federer did not hesitate to credit Annacone for rebuilding his confidence and contributing something valuable to his game. Yet Federer clearly did not want to overshadow Severin's help over the years. Whenever he was asked to reflect on his good form during the period, he did not hesitate to mention Severin. 'I'm sure Paul has helped in this regard. So has Severin. He's helped, as well, over the last few years,' he said in his post-match conference after winning the World Tour Final in 2010. Coaches who feel respected and appreciated are of course more loyal and more willing to dedicate themselves fully to their jobs. Athletes therefore should try to share their glories with their coaches and make them proud.

Competitors: Not many people realise that a significant amount of athletes' career achievements actually come from the push from their competitors. Firstly, competition is no doubt a strong driving force for people to work hard. Secondly, it helps fire up people in order to prevent boredom amid stringent and repetitive daily routine. Thirdly, it provides invaluable information about people's strengths and weaknesses in their respective sports. From a macro perspective, the sports industry needs competition to be appealing. Usually the industry will boom evidently during time of great competition.

In tennis history, rivalry between champions can get rather intense and fractious sometimes. But grateful Federer is able to appreciate and be thankful for his rivalry with Nadal. 'We played on so many occasions, and on so many tough and heated moments, we came out on top; and I think we respected each other immensely and actually almost appreciated the other guy for being there and pushing you to become a better player, and I guess at times even a better person,' Federer said in a press conference during the Indian Wells tournament in 2010. Without Nadal, Federer could have won more French Open titles, broken more records, and felt more at ease at the top. Federer, however, can see the bigger picture beyond winning matches. He is aware that the presence of Nadal is good for maturation of his game as well as for attracting fans and promoting tennis.

Sports legends: For every sport, there were legends in the past. For soccer, we have Pelé, Maradona, Zidane, and so forth. For basketball, we have Magic Johnson, Michael Jordan, and others. For tennis, we have Rod Laver, Boris Becker, Pete Sampras, Steffi Graf, and so forth. For boxing, we have Muhammad Ali, and so on. For snooker, we have Steve Davis, Jimmy White, Stephen Hendry, and more. The list goes on and on. Those were the names repeatedly mentioned in the sports industry. Their legendary stories have inspired younger generations, both inside and outside the industry. All previous legends contributed to the prospering of their respective sports fields. They drew more audiences into the sports with their extraordinary performances. They created records and benchmarks for the followers to look up to. Some even led a paradigm shift in how people played or saw the sport. So for both athletes and the fans, we ought to be grateful that we have those sports legends in the past.

We've heard many nice words from Federer about the tennis legends. He has always been an enthusiastic fan of the legends. I believe it has been primarily driven by his true appreciation of them as great players and perhaps, more importantly, his gratefulness towards their significant contributions to the game. When John McEnroe interviewed him after he tied Sampras's record of fourteen slams by winning the French Open, he thanked Sampras for creating the game and for sticking around for so long to create those records. He appreciates the legends for creating the history of tennis and is obviously pleased that he is now definitely an eminent part of tennis history.

Sports organisers and officials: Regardless of whether the organisers of sports events are true enthusiasts of sports or are opportunistic businesspeople, they help feed the whole industry. They are sometimes mistaken as just sitting there to reap benefits of the industry. No, they invest, secure sponsorships, advertise, and do whatever it takes to put on successful sports events. Similarly, the officials of sports associations do a lot of work behind the scene. They help set the game rules, manage tour schedules, settle disputes, and protect and promote the industry. Unions of sports players put players' welfare as the highest priority and thus of course often run into fights with officials. But as long as they have mutual respect, they are both fighting for the healthy growth of the industry.

Thanks to organisers and officials are usually given in a routine and official manner, such as in ceremonies. Reciprocal actions out of gratitude actually mean more. Back in 1998, Gstaad, a small clay court tennis tournament in Switzerland, offered Federer his first match at the ATP tour level. Years later, Federer turned up at the tournament (as a Wimbledon Champion) for two consecutive years, in 2003 and 2004. It was widely considered a gesture of thanks. Gstaad had a bad schedule because it happened right after the biggest event in tennis - Wimbledon. In addition, a switch from grass back to clay was not fun for players who went far in Wimbledon. So the participation of the Wimbledon champion in Gstaad for two years was unbelievable for the tournament.

In 2003, after claiming his first slam in Wimbledon, Federer didn't just turn up at Gstaad but also gave his best effort to match through the rounds he could possibly play until he lost in five sets in the final. 'I really wanted to win this for you because the way you have received me here has touched me greatly,' Federer said in front of the crowd, expressing his gratitude.

Before the Tennis Masters Cup in Shanghai in 2005, Federer helped promote the event by playing two sets of tennis with the organisers and officials at the centre court of the new stadium. He also gave as many interviews as he could and spent enough time with the officials and fans. He even thanked the cook in person after the dinner. 'Tennis has given me so much that I'm convinced that I should give something back in return. It's not a must for me, but it makes me feel much better,' Federer said.

Fans: If athletes fail to appreciate the support from fans, they will be in big trouble. Arrogance does not earn you more fans. Some take fan support for granted because they believe they have earned it, considering fans only part of the reward for their excellence. All right, that's partly true. Of course, when you have talent and are good at what you do, you deserve to be admired. However, it is definitely not one-sided but should be a give-and-take relationship. Fans do give back a lot. They buy tickets. They are amazing spectators who create the atmosphere needed for an exciting match. They give their loudest cheers and applause to boost up their heroes. They give invaluable consolation and support to their favourites in difficult times. Truly grateful athletes should acknowledge the importance of fans in supporting their careers. Gratitude can help an athlete turn fan support into a driving force for success.

Federer is considered one of the most beloved and cherished athletes among fans. The adoration he received from fans is unmatched across different sports and countries. As a fan of Federer,

I can say that one of the reasons he is so adored is that we, as fans, feel we are treated as valuable assets by Federer. Federer said he valued the time he was running around for players' autographs when he was a ball boy. He remembered how happy and inspired he was as a fan. That's one of the reasons that he has always been so approachable to fans. He answered a question about his setting up a Facebook account: 'It's been nice, and I like to interact. They mean a lot to me that they support me so much – maybe not only on [the] Internet, but also [in] the stadium. I can feel that. It's a way to thank them.'

Some people might argue that gratitude goes against striving for success, saying that when people feel content, they may lose motivation to achieve something bigger in their lives. I think Federer's having both gratefulness and legendary success disputes such arguments. 'I've always dreamt of winning Wimbledon, of being number one in the world, of leading the rankings, and I have to enjoy these moments. You should never forget how thankful you should be to the sport,' Federer said in 2005. 'Federer is the rare superstar who doesn't define himself by his talent but still feels a constant responsibility and gratitude for it,' Justin Gimelstob, a retired American tennis player, wrote in his sports blog for *Sports Illustrated* in 2008.[6] Federer is grateful for his every big win because he understands that one injury can end his career at any time. Gratitude has helped Federer savour his good moments and live through his tough moments.

When he lost to Marat Safin in the Australian Open in 2005, Federer said, 'The more success you have, the easier it is to deal with defeat. I didn't think too much about it even the next day. I woke up; the sun was shining. Sure, my foot was hurting, but there was nothing to worry about. I hadn't been robbed or attacked. Everyone I cared for was fine. It was not a question of blocking out the defeat; I just accepted having to live with the fact and, really, that's not too difficult.' This illustrated how Federer eased himself through defeats. Such mentality apparently has worked very well for Federer throughout the years.

In 2008, Federer lost an epic Wimbledon final to Nadal. He was grateful enough to find positivity in the experience. He said, 'I appreciate that tennis went up a notch with that match, and that's what I strove to do in my five years as number one, to make tennis better, more popular, and I admit that that Wimbledon final achieved all I had wanted, even if I lost it.'

Gratitude is not a hindrance but a crucial ingredient to success. As we give back, we generate more willpower for ourselves to achieve what we want and what we owe to others. When we remember how blessed we are, we will not be let down that hard by adversities. So why not start doing something good for our well-being by learning how to become more grateful?

❖❖❖❖❖❖❖❖❖❖❖❖❖❖❖❖❖❖❖❖❖❖❖❖❖❖

Cultivating gratitude

Grateful people experience more positive emotions, are more satisfied with their lives, are more vital and optimistic, and are more immune to stress. So why don't we learn to be more grateful? And why don't we open ourselves up to greater appreciation of life? To do this, we have to forgo ungrateful attitudes, nurture grateful attitudes, and establish practices of expressing our gratitude.

Remove what is blocking us from being grateful:
The major inhibiting factors for gratefulness are sense of entitlement, preoccupation with materialism, and lack of self-reflection. Sense of entitlement makes us take things for granted

and thus unable to take things as gifts or blessings. Preoccupation with materialism significantly limits our scope and depth of appreciation. Lack of self-reflection makes us too self-sufficient, causing us to easily miss things we should be thankful for. Please try to remove the above blockage, which may stand in your way, to become a grateful person.

Nurturing grateful attitudes:
To bring out your deeper sense of gratitude and make your gratitude more dispositional rather than situational, you need to nurture grateful attitudes in your everyday life. Here are the key constituents of a grateful mindset:

- *Self-contentment*: Be appreciative of and satisfied with what you already have. Reducing upward comparisons and increasing downward comparisons can lead to more self-contentment.
- *Appreciative*: Be less judgemental concerning yourself and others. Instead, try to open up yourself to appreciation of things, people, and experiences. Increase your awareness of good deeds from others, which you might have taken for granted.
- *Empathy and perspective taking*: In interpersonal relationships, empathy and perspective taking can help you be less self-focused and thus more appreciative of others' contributions.

Establishing practices to express gratitude:

- *Gratitude list*: Find a good time to sit down and write a list of things that you feel grateful for over your whole life.

- *Gratitude diary:* Every day write down three good things that happened during the day and think about why/who/what made those good things happen.
- *Act on gratitude:* Be more proactive in expressing your gratitude to others. Take the opportunity to express your thanks to others by sending messages, paying visits, buying gifts of thanks, or offering your help.

❖❖❖❖❖❖❖❖❖❖❖❖❖❖❖❖❖❖❖❖❖❖❖❖❖

Savouring

Happiness in the present moment is often experienced as pleasure. Pleasures are more about positive sensations we naturally feel in positive moments. They usually do not last very long and fade or habituate with time. Savouring is a process that calls for our full awareness of pleasure and conscious attention to the experience of pleasure. It can deepen daily pleasures to enhance one's enduring happiness. To savour, we have to get ourselves oriented in the present. Happy people live mostly for today. They do not spend too much time ruminating negative things in the past, nor do they spend too much time reliving the glories of the good old days. Worrying or idealising about the future is not a significant part of their lives either. They focus more on the here and now.

When people do recreational sports, some focus more on the results, such as losing weight, releasing stress, strengthening muscles or whatever have you. They may underrate a very important benefit of doing sports: experiencing positive feelings before, during, and after doing sports. From my own experiences, here I suggest some of the ways to savour. For example, before playing tennis with my husband or friends, I try to heighten my feelings of anticipation by, let say, preparing the gears attentively, thinking about the strategies or any new things to try out, remembering the fun I had the last time I did it. During playing, we give ourselves fist pumps and call out 'Great shot', 'Yes', 'Yeah', and so forth when executing good shots. This allows us to feel more excitement and satisfaction. After earning tough points or chasing balls from impossible positions, I take some time to appreciate my effort and persistence. Of course, for a recreational activity, we can make it fun by telling jokes or trying trick shots. After playing, we savour the feelings of gratification. We evaluate improvements we've made and how well we tried out new tactics or skills.

In the professional sports industry, people are naturally more result oriented. Victories are the moments to savour. Even so, some people move too fast to the next step, thinking about upcoming competition, without paying enough time to taste their victories. Savouring is not a common topic at all in sports psychology. Evidence may not be strong enough to prove that savouring is effective in improving sporting performance of an athlete. But savouring definitely helps athletes to perceive that they are having good and happy careers, thus giving them the strength to persist.

With all the achievements year after year, instead of habituating, Federer has become more aware of the need for savouring. Federer understands that no title he has won was as easy as it might have seemed. Though he has always been optimistic in the face of increasing challenges from younger players, he has been aware that his edge or even his career can cease in any moment due to injury or something else. So he seizes every opportunity to savour pleasure from his wins.

'It's important for my mind, it's important for my life that I enjoy victories more today than I did in the beginning. Before, I won and I would race to the next tournament, today I try to stay with those victories much more,' he said in an interview with Reuters in 2009.[7] When he matched Pete Sampras's total of sixty-four career titles after taking the title in the Stockholm Open in 2010, he said, 'You never know when it's your last one. That's why you want to savour every tournament victory.' In the press conference right after Federer and Wawrinka won the Beijing Olympics doubles gold medal, someone took the chance to ask Federer about his feeling towards the expected loss of his number one ranking. Federer refused to be guided away from absorbing his great moment. He held the gold model up and said with a smile, 'This feels good. That's my feeling right now.'

How does Federer savour his victories? He said in a post-match conference after claiming his thirteenth major title in the US Open, 'I've gotten in the habit of, if I win a slam, I want to enjoy it first with all my friends and family who came here and supported me throughout. I used to make the error of going into doping control and press right away, and I wouldn't be back for two and a half hours, and then people had to leave, and I wouldn't see them. I give myself a chance to soak up the great moment and enjoy it with them – glass of champagne, be myself for an hour, for a little bit in the locker room. Everybody's so happy. You talk about the match again, about the tournament, how great it is to be sitting here now with the trophy, take all sorts of pictures with the trophy. Everybody's happy and proud. It's a nice moment. I'd like to take my time with that.'

Aside from being nice, I guess one of the reasons Federer spends so much time with the press, especially after his big wins, is that he values the task as a savouring process through analysing the match and reflecting on his feelings with a group of people who care about tennis. Federer also has a habit of watching the highlights of his match and reading newspaper commentaries about his victories. We have so far learned from Federer several effective ways of savouring: absorption in the moment, sharing with others, and snapping pictures of memorable moments.

For athletes, there are some extra chances for savouring – for example, from those polls and awards. There are awards like player of the year, sportsmanship awards, awards voted, by experts and awards voted by fans. Those not only serve as recognitions of players but are also great opportunities for players to savour what they have achieved over the year. Of all the awards, Laureus World Sportsman of the Year is perhaps the most honourable award for athletes due to its global status and the involvement of athletes from all kinds of sports. Federer won Laureus World Sportsman of the Year four times consecutively, from 2005–2008. Federer was happy to receive such recognition, and more than that, he regarded it as a savouring opportunity, as the award allowed him to look back and realise that he really did have an extraordinary year to remember. Federer has a trophy room at home for all the Grand Slam trophies, the Masters Series trophies, and the other awards. He said he had a great feeling every time he was in the trophy room, where he recaptured the feelings of having so much success in his tennis career.

Unfortunately, people often learn to treasure the present moments in a hard way. We have heard many people's awakening stories after having an illness, accidents, and the loss of beloved ones. Tragedies make people aware that taking things for granted is one of the stupidest things to do. Federer learnt more deeply about how important living in the moment should be from the death of Peter Carter, his beloved coach. 'Early in my career, I used to get really upset over a bad shot or something like that, and I couldn't get it out of my head, and it would cost me matches sometimes. Now I've learnt to forget about it, stay calm, and focus on what I'm doing now. Since Peter's death, I try to think about what I'm doing right now,' he said in an interview with ESPN in 2008.[8] 'I learnt that tomorrow isn't promised to anyone,' he added. Psychologically, he tries to play his tournaments very much in the present tense. During a match, he believes the right approach is to think only about the moment that he plays for a point, not to think ahead to the next match or think about the last point. Given the notable attention being paid to the records in the tennis field, Federer finds no way to stay away from being questioned about his chance of keeping the streak or breaking another record. Federer is aware of those records and loves to have them, but during the tournaments, he cares more about the match he is playing and the opponents he is competing against.

Hopefully, we do not need to learn our lessons in a hard way. Starting now, we should all try to live a little bit more in the present and try our very best to savour our good moments.

❖❖❖❖❖❖❖❖❖❖❖❖❖❖❖❖❖❖❖❖❖❖❖❖❖

Savouring techniques

Fred B. Bryant and Joseph Veroff of Loyola University are leaders in research work on savouring. They have proposed five major techniques that promote savouring:

- Sharing with others: Be more proactive in telling others about your positive experiences. When you share your positive moments, you may give a bit more detail on how you feel, what make those moments so special, and how much you value those moments.

- Memory building: Your memories of positive events can be strengthened by imprinting mental images, taking photographs, writing them down, or even getting some physical souvenirs of the events. You may recall those memories from time to time and share them with others.
- Self-congratulation: Do not hesitate to give yourself words of praises or congratulations. You may take in some pride whenever there is a chance, especially in those moments when you are doing a good job.
- Sharpening perceptions: Focus on certain elements of the events and block out other details.
- Absorption: Let yourself get fully immersed in the good moments. Please focus on your sensations, not the thinking.

Establishing savouring practices:
Integrating savouring experience into your daily routine:

- Spare fifteen minutes every day to build a memory of daily positive experiences.
- Share your positive experiences with others when you have a chance. Don't wait too long.
- Develop a regular practice of reviewing photographs or videos.
- Every week plan an activity that is pleasurable to you.

❖❖❖❖❖❖❖❖❖❖❖❖❖❖❖❖❖❖❖❖❖❖❖❖❖❖

Optimism and hope

When we feel optimistic and hopeful, we are feeling good right now due to an expectation of a desirable future. Optimistic people have a tendency to believe that things will get better or current fortune will carry on well into the future. What differentiates between optimism and pessimism is the explanatory style. Pessimists tend to explain unfortunate events in three dimensions: permanence, pervasiveness, and personalization – that is, believing that causes of negative experiences are permanent and pervasive, and the ones to blame are themselves. In contrast, optimists believe that negative events are only specific incidents that happen occasionally and can be attributed to some external factors. The optimistic explanatory style for good events is just the opposite. Optimists believe fortunate events have internal, universal, and permanent causes.

With strong supporting evidence, optimism is found to be significantly related to happiness, better physical health, and more satisfying social relationships. When we are optimistic, we tend to expect and then seek out pleasurable experiences, which in turn reinforces our optimistic logic. Expectation of a favourable outcome enables an optimist to do things that more likely lead to the favourable outcome.

Optimism and hope go hand in hand. Optimism helps cultivate hope for future. Hope is also future-minded and involves three components: goals, willpower, and way power. A goal is something we want to achieve or we desire to do or to have. Willpower is the driving force and motivation behind our goal attainment. Way power is our ability to devise pathways in meeting our goals. When we are hopeful, we are more engaged in life. Hope helps us get past hurdles and move forward. It keeps our aspirations alive.

Optimism and hope may not guarantee achievement in sports, but it surely helps an athlete to be more resilient, to be able to rebound quickly from adversities. The most usual adversities in sports are defeats and injuries. Defeats happen a lot before an athlete finally achieves a career breakthrough. Even at the top, athletes normally still have to face defeats from time to time, maybe because of their occasional lapses. How they appraise defeats, therefore, has a deterministic effect on whether they can maintain overall positive attitudes towards their careers.

A pessimistic explanation for defeats involves much self-blame or self-defeating thoughts, such as 'I played the match completely in a wrong way' and 'I wasn't good enough to do this.' A pessimist tends to generalise the defeats: 'I am a failure,' 'It was the end of my peak or even my career,' and 'My physical body is going downhill from here.' These clearly have adverse impact on one's career by damaging one's will and confidence to achieve goals. Such generalised negative self-perceptions may actually have bad influences on one's other areas of life too, like feeling insecure in relationships or becoming hesitant in making life decisions.

So how to remain optimistic and hopeful despite letdowns? Let us put the psychological theories aside for a while and see how our flourished champion dealt with his tough moments. One of the toughest situations Federer undertook in his entire tennis career was his four consecutive defeats to Nadal in the French Open from 2005 to 2008. One was in the semi-finals, and three were in the finals. There were several legitimate reasons for building pessimism in his chance of getting a French crown.

Firstly, at that time, only five male players had achieved career Grand Slams, that is winning all four grand slams, in the open era. Secondly, for all those years, the French Open has been dominated by baseline players with deep and penetrating groundstrokes. Many ex–world number one players who had good attacking games like Federer and a great resume of slams did not win the French Open no matter how hard they tried and how well they played in the other slams. This included names like Pete Sampras, John McEnroe, and Boris Becker. Thirdly, Rafael Nadal had dominated the clay court for so long and so convincingly, as nobody ever did. He was called the best clay court tennis player of all time. His early success had a head-on collision with Federer's dominant period. Nadal remained the man to beat in the French Open and was crowned for four consecutive years, from 2005 to 2008.

Despite the above facts, Federer refused to be discouraged and remained optimistic about his chance of winning the French Open Slam one day. Year after year, he was knocked down in the French Open finals. Instead of putting his head down, he recognised the significant implication of his reaching the finals, that he had the right game and chance to win the title. While he was aware that achieving this particular goal grew harder with time, he remained hopeful. He believed his job was just to hang in there for as long and as consistently as possible to keep his chance alive. He finally did take the chance in 2009 and won the French Open Slam, the one that had eluded him for years. Even though he had particularly strong motivation to complete his career Grand Slam, he did not get obsessed with it and did not view it as the only thing left to accomplish in his career. He preferred to look at a much bigger picture of his career.

Let us go into Federer's optimistic mind a bit further, particularly his attitude towards defeats. Federer lost a few times to Nadal on clay courts in the first half of the 2006 season before they met again for the Wimbledon final. When people cast doubts about his chance of defeating Nadal in the grass court final, Federer responded, '[Nadal's] beaten me a few times already, but that was on his surface; that shouldn't affect our matches on grass or hard courts. One shouldn't be discouraged by defeats.' Federer believed that the factors behind his defeats were somewhat specific or situational and should not be generalised to the extent that it impaired his hope and confidence in future matches.

Federer has been able to view his losses in positive ways. Sometimes he did feel sorry for missing too many chances or not being able to execute his game. But on more occasions, he admitted that he lost to a better man on that day. We heard him saying that he played badly on a certain day but seldom heard him questioning his own game, saying something like 'I am a bad player'.

In early 2008, Federer suffered a semi-final loss in the Australian Open. It was easy for him to get over it, as his sickness – mononucleosis – could apparently be claimed for the loss. What was more difficult to take was the later back-to-back loss to Nadal in the French Open and the Wimbledon finals. That was widely regarded as a warning sign of career decline at that time. Some even doubted Federer could ever win another slam again. As a normal human being, Federer was disappointed and frustrated. But he never sounded as if he was in despair. He remained hopeful. 'Now I have so many dreams to chase – the French Open, an Olympic singles gold medal in London in 2012, the Davis Cup for Switzerland – but the most important thing is I have to enjoy it,' he said. Then he added, 'I believe I can do this as long as I'm healthy, and I will believe as long as my tennis days [continue] that I can win a Grand Slam. If it's not the case, I will probably retire. But I believe that for a very long time to come, I still believe I will win Wimbledon, I still believe I will win the US Open; and I still believe I will win the French Open; I truly think it should not be a problem having a shot there because I am such a good all-rounder.'[9]

Federer never loses track of his goals. He understands what the goals mean to him and believes in his chances of attaining the goals. His motivation and determination have perhaps been his most threatening weapons. Over the years, he has shown a strong will to succeed and achieve more. He carefully plans ways to attain his goals. He takes charge of his own practice and tournament schedule. He seeks professional help from a conditioning trainer and physiotherapist when needed. He plans his media and sponsorship duties without losing track of his top priority, which is playing good tennis. Equipped with the above qualities, Federer never feel hopeless.

No matter which career we are in, sport or non-sport, we should try to take unfortunate events more lightly. Instead of kicking ourselves hard, we can have a fair evaluation of what went wrong. Apart from fixating on our own faults, we'd better also think about some external or specific factors that might have caused the results. In doing so, we are not finding excuses for ourselves but having a more thorough evaluation that prevents us from getting too pessimistic solely because of one unfortunate incident. Remember not to generalise a disappointing performance in one area to other areas, saying such things as 'I am not successful in this. Therefore, I am a failure and won't be successful in anything in the future'. This kind of thought is harmful. We have to stop making those unnecessary negative associations.

When something good happens, we may try attributing it to enduring factors that are likely to repeat in the future. We should avoid minimising our own successes. We should take the credits we deserve. We may spend some time thinking about how we can repeat our success in the future or make it happen in other areas of life too. To remain hopeful, we need to keep good track of our goals and have strong belief in our ability to attain our goals. Not to be mistaken, I am not suggesting that we should be positive about everything as if wearing blindfolds. Somehow we just need a more balanced assessment of the real situations in order to build hope and optimism about the future.

✧✧✧✧✧✧✧✧✧✧✧✧✧✧✧✧✧✧✧✧✧✧✧✧✧✧✧✧

Enhancing optimism and hope

To strengthen your optimistic thinking, you might practice the following mental exercise.

When you encounter difficulty or negative experience:

- Identify if you have any pessimistic thoughts on the incident.
- Examine your dimension of attributions, whether it is too permanent, pervasive, or personalised.
- Realistically reattribute causes to some more transient, specific, and/or external factors.
- Ask yourself if anything good came from the experience.
- Ask yourself what you have learned from the experience.

When positive thing happens to you:

- Look for any personal contribution that has made the thing happen.

- Look for any reasons that the positive experience will repeat in the future.
- Look for sustainable positive impact from the experience.

Instillation of hope can be done by doing 'the best possible selves' exercise:

- Think of your best possible future self in two years, five years, or ten years.
- In your projections, try to cover as many major life domains that you care about.
- The exercise can be done as a write-up or a mental image.

❖❖❖❖❖❖❖❖❖❖❖❖❖❖❖❖❖❖❖❖❖❖❖❖

While we emphasise the significance of experiencing positive emotions, we have to be careful not to reject our negative emotions. In psychology, we largely acknowledge the adaptive functioning of negative emotions. For example, fear helps one escape from danger, anxiety helps one take necessary precautions, anger helps one be alert when others violate one's own rights, and so forth. Invalidating such emotions can be damaging to our psychological health. We need to accept and acknowledge our negative emotions as much as we embrace our positive emotions.

CHAPTER 3
Engagement (E)

Sporting flow experience

Have you ever been so engaged in a process or activity that you felt yourself fully absorbed in the moment? Wasn't such an experience wonderful and gratifying? This, what we usually call 'in the zone' state, is defined as flow in positive psychology. Flow describes an optimal experience of full immersion in what one's doing. It is a subjective feeling with certain key characteristics, as identified by Nakamura and Csíkszentmihalyi, the pioneers in flow research.[10] Here are the six markers of flow:

- Intense and focused concentration on the present moment
- Merging of action and awareness
- Loss of reflective self-consciousness
- Sense of personal control or agency over the situation or activity

- Distortion of temporal experience; one's subjective experience of time is altered
- Experience of the activity as intrinsically rewarding

Please note that the presence of pleasure is not a definitive feature of flow. Pleasure is more of a momentary positive feeling that habituates quickly over time. In a 'doing mode', the experience of flow may not be emotional at all. Gratified feelings often kick in after the flow has stopped. Gratification is derived from enactment of personal strength that leads to personal growth. It has benefits that are even more enduring. Gratification encourages commitment and persistence, particularly in facing challenging tasks. Relevant skills are enhanced as a result, as is self-confidence. Despite the benefits of gratification, many people often choose pleasure over gratification in their everyday lives because the wealthy society has created so many shortcuts to experience pleasure easily, whether it's watching TV, shopping, pleasurable entertainment, or even drugs. For the sake of our well-being, we have to engage ourselves more in activities that bring us gratification rather than short-lived pleasure.

Almost all types of sports, especially during competitions, require players to be in a highly concentrated state. Somehow, as spectators, we sense it when the professional players are playing in the zone. The intensity of focusing is well shown in their facial expressions and body postures. Their movements are so smooth and natural, displaying a perfect fusion of mind and body. They appear to be in full control of exhibiting their repertoire of tactics and skills. While flow is an optimal and satisfying experience psychologically, it does not necessarily bring out peak performance every time. However, when they coincide, those magical moments are exceptionally gratifying.

Federer's semi-final match against Andy Roddick in the 2007 Australian Open was a great example. The result – winning 6–4, 6–0, 6–2 – was no doubt incredible. But it was the way he played the match that was most astonishing. He hit the balls with so much precision and power. He had an answer to every tactic Roddick imposed on him. Everything seemed to be working for him: forehands, backhands, and the reflective half-volleys. One of the commentators of the match described his own perceptual distortion: the court appeared to be smaller on Federer's side than Roddick's. Maybe it was because Federer's excellent anticipation helped him get to the right positions to hit the balls early. Anyway, what we saw was a peak performance. But we could not observe flow. Only Federer could feel the intensity of flow he had. When Federer was asked to describe the experience in the post-match on-court interview, he used the word 'unreal'.

Even though a sport is usually a highly engaging activity, not all people experience flow every time they are doing sports. Surely, the most important prerequisite is to have a genuine interest in the sport; otherwise, the rewarding feeling will not be intrinsic. There are also other preconditions for a flow state to occur. For example, it makes quite a difference whether you are doing the sport for fun or making it a goal-directed activity. Now let us look at some general factors for achieving a flow state: [11]

- We should know what to do and have a clear set of goals.
- We should know how to do something with clear directions and plans.
- The task should give clear and immediate feedback.
- The task should be free from distractions.
- There should be a good balance between the perceived challenges of the task and the perceived skill level. (A

combination of highly perceived challenge and medium-to-high skill level is set for creating flow experience. One will be stressed out if she has to deal with a challenging task with a relatively low skill level. Or the other way round, one will feel bored if she has to deal with a task that involves a low level of challenge relative to her own skill level.)

We can seek opportunities for experiencing flow from a great many everyday activities, like working, reading, painting, cooking, you name it, as long as we know how to satisfy the above preconditions. In the sporting world, athletes, coaches, and sports psychologists should study factors that lead to flow experience and thus try to optimise the conditions in training and competitions that enable athletes to experience such optimal experience. The gratifications thereby increase an athlete's self-belief, perseverance, and commitment, which are invaluable factors for achieving success in sports. We know why, and now we need to see how. Considering the above preconditions for sports, the following advice should work for both professional and recreational sports players:

1. Set clear goals on your tasks and activities
   This isn't referring to setting long-term goals. Of course, we need that too. But considering flow, we are concerned with moment-by-moment experiences. Therefore, we need to set clear goals on an activity basis in order to open ourselves up for flow experience. We ought to set goals for individual matches or training. If we can make regular training and exercise an optimal experience for us,

we are definitely enjoying an edge over others in achieving long-term goals.

2. Devise concrete plans and execute them decisively

   Concrete plans need to be devised according to the goals. While input from others, such as coaches, trainers, physiologists, or psychologists, is helpful, an athlete should play a significant role in making his own plans because feeling of ownership is important in the optimization process. Flow requires decisive execution of the plans. For example, a tennis player usually comes to a match with a clear game plan. A changing game plan during the match is sometimes needed and helps win the match. But 'in the zone' performances are usually generated from full execution of the same plan right from the beginning to the end.

3. Pay attention to immediate feedback, non-judgementally

   Most of the tasks involved in sports give us immediate feedback. For example, in ball games, the direction and the speed of the ball provide a lot of information on how well we strike the ball, no matter we are using rackets, our bare hands, our feet or our heads. For track and field sports, the speed, power, direction and distance we make with our body movements tell us to adjust accordingly for our next motions. Paying attention to immediate feedback is necessary for a flow state to occur. Yet the most crucial and difficult part is to do it non-judgementally. An athlete in the zone only sees the feedback as information to keep doing what's working, making necessary adjustments for the next move. Too many judgements in evaluating the feedback – e.g., judging the shots or moves as good, bad, or lousy – triggers unnecessary emotions that will bring us out of the zone.

4. Perceive the activity as a challenge and master it with self-belief

Athletes with higher self-confidence are more prone to flow experiences, especially during matches. On the one hand, they perceive competitions as challenging. On the other hand, they believe they can master the challenges with their skills. But they may find it harder to feel the same in trainings, as they fail to perceive them as challenging. They have to learn to view training not only as routine practice but also challenges for them to conquer and to sharpen their skills. Players with lesser self-confidence often overestimate the challenges or underestimate their own levels of skills. Both make flow less probable. So remember, you should try to believe in yourself in executing your plan and displaying your skills to overcome the challenges, whether you are in a training, practice match, or real match.

5. Focus on here and now; resist distractions

Distractions interrupt flow, and once the process is disturbed, it's rather hard for people to revert back into the zone. Therefore, the ability to concentrate has to be trained and enhanced so that the athlete can stay focused when dealing with all possible sources of distractions, due to weather conditions, loud spectators, and unexpected incidents. Besides, the focus needs to be put on here and now – on the process, not the result. More often, the distractions come from our own minds. When we fixate on the results, we are simply not in a being mode. Tennis players often share that the right way to approach a match is to play shot by shot, point by point, though not many can really do as they wish. They try not to think about previous shots they made, whether they were bad or magnificent. They also try not to think ahead too much, even when they are on the verge of winning or losing.

6. Explore and cultivate intrinsic motivation

   Motivation has to come from within, based on intrinsic rather than extrinsic rewards. In sports, extrinsic rewards are usually money, getting attention, showing off talent, living with fame, and so on, while intrinsic rewards are more about mastering the skills, riding on the learning curve, and actualising the potential. We shouldn't let extrinsic rewards cover up our deeper and inner drive, because only if we nurture our intrinsic motivation can we experience the beauty of flow.

Passion and vitality

Anther way to look at how engaging our lives are is to see how much and how often we feel passionate about things happening in our lives. Passion describes a strong feeling of eagerness, enthusiasm, and desire towards a person or a thing. This emotion gives us high energy and the compelling urge to approach our goals. Successful sports players are usually very passionate. They show more love for their sports than their peers do. Passion, more than anything, is the major motivational push for them. For example, tennis is a sport that does not have much of an off season. Players have to travel from one tournament to another across different cities and countries almost throughout the year. Maintaining a high level of energy, enthusiasm, and motivation is a key ingredient for performance consistency.

Federer clearly has had so much passion for the game all along, which I believe has made a profound contribution to his stunning accomplishments. Despite his calmness and restrained emotions on court, his passion was manifested impressively on many occasions. One of the most remembered moments perhaps was Federer's painful tears after his brutal loss to Nadal in the 2009 Australian Open final. After the match, he did not get a chance to calm himself down privately. He found himself stuck at the court and later lost his composure in front of the crowds at the trophy ceremony. His voice trembled, and he started to shed tears after uttering the first few words. He had to delay his speech as a result. Nadal later put his arm around Federer's shoulder to console him.

The scene aroused different opinions. Somebody took it as a moment of embarrassment and the meltdown of a king. Somebody was touched by it and loved it. I was obviously one of those who felt deeply touched by Federer's passion in the game and by the mutual respect between the top two players. Federer himself believed the emotion reflected his feelings for the game. 'You love tennis, and you get emotional because the fans are into it and you feel like you're so close, and all of a sudden you realise you're so far again. So this is what brought out the tears ... I still believe it shows that there is a human side to, I mean, any player because we care about this game and try hard,' Federer said.

Passionate sports players are different from so-so ones in many ways. The energy and eagerness inside can drive such players to do much more than they are expected to do, such as the following:

They sustain a high level of participation and never want to quit. Passion gives us enough energy to maintain a high level of participation in the sport for a long time. For example, Lionel

Messi has been known as a passionate footballer since childhood. Almost all the people in his family, and even in his country, are football enthusiasts. When young, he always played with his ball and was the last to leave the training field. Now, as the most valued player in FC Barcelona, even in the world, he has an incredibly high participation rate in matches. He plays full matches in almost all matches. Once he is on the field, he hates to be called off. He doesn't like sitting on the bench watching the game. He is usually the most eager one to get back on the field after injuries.

In the tennis field, professionals are as impressed by Federer's passion for the game as they are impressed by his talent. Now, at the age of thirty-two (as of this writing), he has been on the professional tour for almost two decades and has played over one thousand matches. He is the only player, among the top players, who never retires from a match in play. He only retired from a tournament (a walkover) once. Rowing with Federer's difficulties in performance, particularly in recent years, there have been waves of predictions or speculations about Federer's retirement from his tennis career. But we never hear Federer himself saying that he is getting sick of the game or losing his motivation or anything that shows the slightest sign that he has lost his passion for the game.

Rene Stauffer, who wrote a biography about Federer, once said, 'His motivation is bigger than ever. It's something astonishing for me. He's talking now about trying to play until he's thirty-five. He's not really driven by records ... He just can't get enough of tennis. He stays up late and watches other guys playing on TV. He's really just a tennis nut.'[12]

John McEnroe was also amazed by Federer's hunger for the sport even after he became a new father of twin girls in 2009. He said, 'One of the important things he has over everyone, and he has it more than any other player I've seen since Connors, is his love for the sport. Real love. He loves to be out there, to be around tennis, everything about it' (from the *Times*).

Nick Fustar, the coach of a young player who got lucky to have chance to practice with Federer in Dubai in early 2008, wrote the following in his blog: 'He [Federer] genuinely enjoyed every minute of practice. I was impressed at the amount of fun that this guy, who happens to have won twelve Grand Slams, had during a two-hour practice session.'

Paul Annacone became Federer's coach in 2010, when the twenty-nine-year-old champion tried to find new height in the late stage of his career. Annacone did not want to coach a player who was merely driven by frustration or resentment of not catching up with younger guys, as is the case for many athletes at the ends of their careers. After a trial coaching period with Federer, Annacone completely dropped his concern and delightedly assumed the duty of coaching Federer. In just a few trial training days, Annacone was impressed by Federer's genuine passion for the game, saying, 'For us to get together took all of about two days of [my] spending time with him in Zurich, training and seeing that he was like a twenty-two-year-old. We were doing three-and-a-half-hour training sessions on the court, and he was smiling and laughing and doing sprints, and I knew that he really loves playing. He isn't playing out of frustration or resentment – it is sheer enjoyment for him.'

Because of his phenomenal career, people apparently find it hard to believe that Federer can still be as enjoyable on the tour when he fell from the top. Federer tried to make the press understand that passion had always been a deeper drive for him and some other players. Here is what he told the press when interviewed during Masters 1000 in Shanghai 2012: 'Sometimes you're just happy playing. Some people, some media, unfortunately don't understand that it's OK just to play tennis and enjoy it. They always think you have to win everything. It always needs to be a success story, and if it's not, obviously what is the point. Maybe you have to go back and think, *Why have I started playing tennis?* Because I just like it. It's actually sort of a dream hobby that became somewhat of a job. Some people just don't get that ever. So for us, the players, it's logical that we love doing what we're doing and ... want to do it as long as [we] can.'

When Federer led the tennis field, involvement of tennis players in Olympic Games has never been as strong, with all top players lined up for the Olympic Games. Federer has an undeniable effect in building enthusiasm among players in the Olympics. Previous tennis champions had only fair participation in the Olympics, which was considered a lesser event than the Grand Slams. Federer, nevertheless, had participated in Olympics four times since his first appearance in the Sydney Olympics in 2000. The line-up for the Olympics has since grown stronger and stronger, almost matching that of a Grand Slam tournament.

The Swiss was well rewarded for his passion in the Olympics. He won a gold medal in doubles with Wawrinka in the Beijing Olympics in 2008, pumping his spirit up after a disappointing loss in a Wimbledon final. The silver medal he won in singles in the 2012 London Olympics might not be perfect for him, but it was enough to give him an emotional moment to remember. He said, 'Every Olympics has been a life changer for me, to be quite honest, in Sydney, in Athens, and Beijing. Good or bad, I think I took away many positives, from the Olympic spirit... I love watching sports because of the reactions of the people at the very end. How do they take wins? How do they take losses?

All these things. For me, it's always been a dream to be part of the Olympic spirit.'

They embrace everything that goes with the sport. When people are really into a sport, they should hope that the intensity of their passion can be strong enough to make them enjoy all the things that go with the sport. They don't want their enthusiasm to be impaired bit by bit because they are annoyed about certain things other than the sport itself. Such is the case with Federer. He is compelled by his passion to embrace whatever goes with his tennis career. He's told people many times that he likes almost everything that goes along with tennis. He tries to make his travelling from tournaments to tournaments as enjoyable and as comfortable as he can. Tim Henman, the famous British tennis player, confirmed this: 'He [Federer] looks like he enjoys everything that goes with it. He obviously enjoys the success on court, but he is comfortable with the attention from the fans and the attention in his home country, and I think it is a great asset because there doesn't seem like there are many things that are making him uncomfortable.'[13]

They care about the sport itself, beyond themselves. What makes one a representative of a sport? It's not just about how talented one is or how many wins one has made. It is more about how much one has contributed or is willing to contribute to the development of the sport. Unfortunately, some high achievers in their respective sporting fields do more harm than contribution to their own sports. There is cheating, unfair play, drug use, gambling, verbal attacks on competitors, you name it. We tend to doubt one's passion for a sport if he allows himself to damage it. Passionate athletes bear the responsibility of fostering the flourishing of their own sports, and at the very least, not doing anything harmful to the fields.

Federer has engaged himself fully in the role of representative for the sport. He is asked to give opinions on almost everything related to the game: the other players, the officials, the schedule, the rules, and so on. He devotes much of his time to events that help promote the sport, particularly in areas where tennis is not that popular (e.g., China, other Asian countries, and the Middle East). He became the president of the ATP Player Council in 2008, as voted by the fellow players. For a certain period, there were three top players heading the council, with Nadal and Djokovic being the vice presidents. Such a strong team obviously earned more attention when they represented the players. With Federer leading the team, the council was seriously involved in several major issues about the tour and made the effort to push forward changes to raise the benefits of players. Some players and ex–council members paid tribute to Federer on raising the status of the Player Council.

Federer is particularly concerned about protecting the positive images of tennis. He is the one who calls for more stringent drug tests on players. He tries to avoid bringing up controversies in public and prefers settling disputes away from the spotlight. He wants to unite the whole field to do something positive for the sport as well as for charity.

Federer loves to see other players showing their passion too. When Juan Martin Del Potro defeated Federer and won his first Grand Slam, he was emotional and shed tears during the trophy presentation. Federer thought it was good to see Del Potro being so happy and emotional about it. Andy Murray also shed some tears during his speech at the ceremony after he was defeated by Federer in the Australian Open in 2010. Federer later shared his feeling about that moment: 'In a way, it was hard to watch, but at the same time, I like seeing players who care for the game.'

Vitality refers to a personality strength that empowers one's zest and enthusiasm in life. People who have this strength are energetic and vigorous. They engage fully in their activities with the feeling of self-absorption and devotion. They display much aliveness and passion in their lives. While Federer's vitality is fully manifested in playing tennis, his enthusiasm in life is not limited to it. When he was young, he tried almost every sport, including skiing, swimming, skateboarding, and all sorts of ball games like soccer, basketball, table tennis, and badminton. Even after he chose to dedicate himself to tennis, he retains his interest in watching other sports events. Soccer is obviously one of those. He is into his favourite home team, FC Basel. He even paid a visit to the players of the team. He once went with Thierry Henry, his star soccer friend, to watch an Arsenal's match in London in 2011. He acted like an excited fan by asking Henry all sort of questions about how the players played the match.

Other than sports, Federer enjoys visiting places around the world, seeing different things, and trying food of different cultures. He even took a Mandarin lesson during his Shanghai tournament in 2010. Federer expresses great interest in other people's lives and is becoming increasingly active in charity works. He likes fashion. He is so pleased to have his own family, and he gets involved in taking care of his children as much as he can. Federer's entire life has been very engaged and lively.

Energetic life is derived from good physical health. We can engage ourselves more broadly and deeply in life experiences only when we feel ourselves fit enough to do so. Pain, illness, and fatigue are major inhibitors in limiting our enthusiasm. Therefore, maintaining a healthy lifestyle is significant in building the strength of vitality. Here are some guidelines for establishing a healthy life routine:

- Eat healthily and regularly: have a balanced diet with sufficient nutrients and vitamins; drink enough water; refrain from eating junk food
- Ensure good quality of sleep: have sufficient sleep; sleep at regular hours; ensure comfortable sleeping environment
- Do exercise, particularly aerobic exercises, on a regular basis
- Relax occasionally to release the tension in your mind and muscle
- Don't smoke; avoid too much alcohol or caffeine

Vitality is also associated with effectiveness and autonomy.

- Using our energy effectively enables us to maintain high levels of functioning for longer periods. Being passionate does not mean we have to draw everything out of our bodies every time. We should learn how to obtain the greatest output from minimising our input (i.e., operate optimally). Being effective helps preserving and refreshing our pool of vigour.
- Being autonomous in exploring our own interests and choosing our own life priorities is important for driving our enthusiasm in life. With autonomy, we enjoy more intrinsic motivation in achieving our goals, which makes our effort, devotion, or even sacrifice more justifiable. We should listen more to our hearts to see what sorts of activities or tasks we feel like engaging in.

CHAPTER 4
Positive Relationships (R)

Today's increasingly individualistic and materialistic world gives rise to a mistaken belief that in order to be happy, people need to possess more for their own good. Many people learn hard lessons before realising that obsession with possessions is in fact detrimental to well-being. We hear stories of seriously sick people regretting not spending enough time with family. There are many people complaining about feeling empty and lonely despite filling their lives with high-quality goods. Fortunately, in psychology we never rule out or underestimate the influence of interpersonal relationships. Research studies have helped us realise that relationships are central to our happiness. Positive relationships are accommodating, inspiring, and communicative. Convincing evidence shows that loving, trusting, and supportive relationships are significant contributors to one's physical health and psychological well-being.

Just as everybody does, athletes need to be connected with other people positively in order to feel satisfied with their lives. Sports achievement alone won't be enough to make one feel flourished. The quality of relationships can also affect one's sporting career substantially. I believe we all understand how relationships at our workplaces affect morale. Stability of our personal relationships has an evident influence on our work performance too. In the industry of sports, impact of relationships is magnified. Only a very fine line is drawn between a successful and mediocre athlete. Playing sports demands highly focused dedication in order to succeed, and a little distraction can make a huge difference in performance. When Tiger Woods divorced, his performance dropped instantly, and his ranking kept heading south. He needed a year to come up from his career bottom. Athletes with more stable relationships, including both professional and personal ones, tend to show more consistency and better mental strength throughout their careers.

Professional relationships

The professional network for an athlete is rather extensive, including relationships with officials, coaches, physiotherapists, agents, competitors, audiences, fans, and so on. Whether or not such relationships are satisfying directly influences how athletes progress in their careers. Positive professional relationships help an athlete gain the necessary skills and knowledge to succeed. Moreover, they make one's sporting career more enjoyable and psychologically rewarding.

As an example, let us look at how Federer's coaching relationships helped him develop into a mature tennis player with the qualities of a great champion. Federer's three coaches – Peter Carter, Peter Lundgren, and Tony Roche – contributed positively to Federer's tennis game and, perhaps more importantly, to Federer's attitude towards tennis. Peter Carter probably was the first and most significant one to establish a positive co-worker relationship with Federer. He taught Federer tennis techniques as well as professional manner and attitude. Bob Carter, father of Peter Carter, described Peter as a calm and collected person, and he believed Peter's personality contributed positively to Federer's developing similar qualities, which benefited his tennis as well. Carter appeared to be the perfect person to help shape teenage Federer in positive ways. Carter became Federer's mentor and trusted friend. Despite the fact that they parted from the coaching relationship later on, they remained friends. Federer summed up how Carter influenced him as a player and a man in the press conference during the Indian Wells tournament in 2005. He said, 'He taught me how to be … a gentleman, how to act as a man, and his technique. He played even nicer than I did. [I think I always] tried to play like him a little bit, especially his backhand. I think that's what I take away most from him because he was a great man.' What he did not mention here was Carter's belief in his potential.

Darren Cahill, another famous tennis coach who was a close friend of Carter's, remembered watching Carter coach thirteen-year-old Federer. When Cahill saw Federer as a fairly good player, Carter could not agree and appeared confident that Federer had great potential to be very good, if not great. Carter's confidence in Federer's potential clearly laid solid ground for young Federer to grow more confidence.

Peter Lundgren became Federer's coach in 2000. Lundgren was known as a positive and easy-going guy. On the tennis side, he had experiences in all major tournaments and wanted to pass along to Federer all his knowledge, gaining from his wins as well as losses. He had strong faith in Federer's tennis career all along. Before Federer won his first major at Wimbledon in 2003, people kept wondering why he had not yet won any major despite his talent and striking performance at some other tournaments. Lundgren was determined that Federer would win the major one day and be followed by more. Lundgren's faith in Federer surely had positive influence on Federer's tennis career during their partnership and even after their parting from their coaching relationship.

Federer's third coach, Tony Roche, contributed positively to his game, particularly on volleys and net games. Yet the real chemistry that made the relationship work was some similarities in their personalities. Roche was a polite and modest man. He was also relaxed and laid back. I think this relationship might have reinforced Federer's relaxed style on court and modest and laid-back life off court. Overall, coaching relationships have some defining influences on athletes' development of work ethics and the mindset and sportsmanship of champions.

How are we to build positive relationships around us? There have been abundant studies to investigate this. Well, even common sense has told us a lot. Personality traits such as honesty, humour, integrity, forgiveness, and so on, are certainly relationship enhancing. Social and communication skills have to be good. And it is necessary for us to cultivate trust, understanding, mutual support, and harmony in our relationships. But I am not going to go into details of each of the above because I want to keep things simple. I do want to emphasise the very basic human quality in building relationships: *being nice*.

Kindness and generosity are basic endeavours of humanity. When you are kind and generous, you are generally nice to other people, with compassionate feelings and altruistic acts of doing favours or good deeds for others. You understand and show concerns for the interests and well-being of other people, sometimes even going beyond your own immediate wishes and needs.

For elite athletes who are constantly being praised or even worshiped, it is normal for them to feel a certain degree of self-importance. Federer repeatedly cites this statement as his living motto: 'It's nice to be important, but it's more important to be nice.' Perhaps this best describes an attitude that athletes need to adopt to avoid having their relationships hurt by their own fame. When you are not nice, your sense of self-importance will be taken as arrogance. When you are nice, the sense of self-importance will be respected and seen as self-confidence.

Explaining how to be nice seems a bit awkward. I think everybody knows what is nice and what is not. So I prefer telling stories that hopefully can inspire readers and stimulate some self-reflection. Apart from his stunning achievements in tennis, what has made Federer so unique and eminent is his reputation of being an extremely genial person. He has gained a great deal of his popularity through his nice attitude towards people. He is a rare breed of being a long-time champion who is so well liked by his fellow players, media, officials, and fans. In a round table interview for the 2005 Tennis Masters Cup, a reporter asked Federer how he could be that friendly with everyone. He responded, 'Why should I be unpleasant when I can just as well be nice?' Maybe we should all ask this question of ourselves.

With fellow players: Fellow players admire and respect Federer as a tennis player and like him as a person and friend. It is very much agreed that he is the most popular champion the tennis world has ever had. He can be friends with most of the fellow players. He greets and chats with other players easily in the locker room. He makes positive and generous comments about other players. He almost invariably pays compliments to his opponents, in both his victories and losses. He has been labelled a gracious winner. I have seen many occasions when Federer had only a muted celebration before walking quickly to the net when his opponent suffered a tough loss. The hugs and exchanges of words at the net were genuine and friendly.

People are most amazed by his classy rivalry with Rafael Nadal, who has won fourteen Grand Slam single titles so far. These two players met so many times in the finals, many of which were in the Grand Slam tournaments. The rivalry is supposed to be intense and head-on. However, while you feel the tension between the two on the court, you don't feel hatred or opposition off court. We don't expect to see these two top players attacking each other in their interviews or elsewhere. Despite occasional blows in the air, initiated sometimes by media or fans, they maintain mutual respect for each other and often exchange nice compliments.

They are not close friends, but they chat easily when they meet and exchange text messages sometimes. When Nadal pulled out of the tournament in Basel in 2005 due to an injury, Federer visited him in the hospital. As a friendly gesture, when Nadal had trouble with his flight schedule to his next tournament after 2007's Montreal tournament, Federer offered him a ride on his private jet, and they had a nice lunch and chatted together with their girlfriends. They sent congratulatory messages to each other on some important wins. 'Federer is not only a world's top-ranked player and a great person; he is also quiet, calm, and most importantly, he's nice,' Nadal once said.

Nadal admitted that he cried in the locker room for half an hour after his five-set loss to Federer in the 2007 Wimbledon final. During the trophy presentation, Federer could not emphasise enough that the match was so close. 'I told Rafa at the net he deserved it as well. So I am the lucky one today,' Federer said.

Federer's nice words might serve as a bit of consolation to Nadal. Two years later, Federer earned back Nadal's support. Nadal consoled a weeping Federer at the trophy ceremony of the 2009 Australian Open, where Nadal defeated Federer in a five-set final.

The relationship between these two rivals has almost been too cosy, to the extent that some people started to accuse Federer of losing his edge on court by being too friendly to Nadal. Federer totally disagreed and continued to fight hard against Nadal on court but chose to enjoy the relationship off court with his great rival in his usual friendly way. If being nice to others is his personality trait and guiding principle, I don't think he is going to change that just because some people prefer more fire and demons than harmony.

Nadal suffered a dip in performance, going eleven months without a title, after he incurred an injury during the clay season in 2009. Some of the press started to doubt whether Nadal would ever come back. Federer, who had a similar experience in 2008, empathised with Nadal. He defended Nadal and said it was not right or fair to write off Nadal. He expected him to come back strong. Nadal did come back with convincing wins in the clay season in 2010, earning his fifth French Open trophy and reclaiming the world number one ranking from Federer.

Federer defeated Andy Roddick, a long-time American top tennis player and Federer's earlier rival, brutally in four Grand Slam finals, including the US Open once and Wimbledon three times. Roddick perhaps should be expected to build up a little bit of loathing towards Federer. Yet it was not the case. After Roddick lost to Federer in straight sets in 2005 Wimbledon final, he said, 'I've told him [Federer] before, "I'd like to hate you, but you're really nice."' He showed his respect for how Federer handled himself on and off court. Here was what Roddick told people about Federer in 2005: 'There have been a lot of good champions, but he's just classy. He is never high and mighty in the locker room or anything like that. He treats people with respect. Even if it's the locker room attendants or the people serving food, he is "please" and "thank you". I think that's why he's so well liked on tour. There's not a whole lot of animosity towards him, even though he has been that successful.'

Roddick could become very challenging and bad-mouthed towards some other players at times. For example, in the 2008 US Open, Roddick lost to Novak Djokovic in the quarter-final match. Roddick apparently accused Djokovic of faking injuries by joking that Djokovic had sixteen injuries and had the bird flu, anthrax, SARS, the common cold, and so forth. Federer, on the other hand, earned Roddick's respect by showing the same level of respect, if not more, towards Roddick. He always had nice comments about Roddick. He even defended Roddick when people started underestimating him or writing him off. He often told others how tremendous it was for Roddick to maintain his top ranking consistently over the years, saying that Roddick deserved more respect. Before Wimbledon 2010 began, Federer again said he admired Roddick's power in staying in contention, saying that Roddick should be respected at Wimbledon. Roddick appreciated Federer's encouragement and said, 'Obviously, that's what you want to hear from one of your peers.' So when people tried to put away Federer after his ranking fell to number three in early 2011, Roddick felt the need to support his friend in return: 'That's ridiculous. I mean, whoever wants to criticise Roger for the way he's playing tennis right now better be very, very good at [his] job.'

Many other fellow players have their own little nice stories to tell about Federer: James Blake, another American player, had a seriously injured neck in 2004. Besides a few American players visiting him, he got a note in hospital from Federer, saying, 'We'll miss you, and we really hope you get back here quickly.' Clearly, Blake welcomed Federer's kind gesture and took this to heart. In a post-match ceremony with Federer two years later, Blake recalled the incident and said that he got one note in the hospital that he still considered special, from Roger Federer. Blake later explained his surprise: 'I had only played him two or three times, but he was thinking of me, and knowing I was alone. He's not only the greatest player; he's the greatest champion this sport could hope for.'

Sam Querrey, an American player of a younger generation, had his career-best season in 2009 by reaching five tour finals and winning one of them. Unfortunately, he got his arm injured in a rare accident, when a glass table fell over, during the last quarter of the season. The injury scared him and kept him resting for the remainder of the season. Querrey heard from other American players, Andy Roddick and James Blake, after the accident, but he was most excited about an email from Federer wishing him well. 'That was the greatest. I was so happy. It made my day. It was almost worth it,' Querrey said.

Marsel Ilhan, a Turkish player, was surprised when he saw Federer approach and congratulate him for becoming the first Turkish man to win a match in a Grand Slam. He could not believe that Federer pay attention to low rank player like him.

Fabrice Santoro, a French tennis player who was on the professional tour for a long time, was asked by the *New York Times* in 2009 to name the most pleasant player on a human level. His reply was prompt: 'No doubt at all: Roger Federer. He's elegant on and off the court, a fine ambassador for tennis.'

During his tour, Federer likes to hang out with other Swiss players, chatting, playing cards, and having fun together. Many

of the Swiss players are his long-time friends. He offers his help
to his Swiss colleagues by giving them advice on their own games
as well as on their opponents'. He sometimes even took time to
cheer for them in the stands.

Michael Lammer was cheered by Federer in the qualifying
rounds of the US Open in 2005 and received advice from Federer
before the match. Federer was happy when his Swiss friends
qualified for the big tournaments and moved through the rounds.
But as he became a bigger and bigger icon, he understood that he
could add a bit of pressure to the Swiss guys if he watched them
play. So he now watches them on TV.

When Federer withdrew from the tournament in Dubai in
2009 due to his back injury, he stayed in Dubai to practice and
fulfil a sponsor responsibility. His two Swiss colleagues, Macro
Chiudinelli and Michael Lammer, made some good moves in the
qualifying and early rounds of the Dubai tournament. Michael
Lammer was a guest at Federer's apartment in Dubai. Lammer
told *Gulf News* after winning his second qualifying rounds, 'Roger
is a good friend, and he has allowed me to stay at his apartment
here. I hope I can compensate this gesture by going as far as
possible in the main draw ... Roger is always there to help any of
us any time. And besides, he is such a great friend too.'

Marco Chiudinelli, who did not stay at Federer's house, said, 'I
have been over to his place, and we had dinner together. It is good
to have him around. Roger is not coming here, but we are in contact
all the time. He is happy that we are doing well.' His friendships
with the Swiss players have gone back a long way. Lammer recalled
a good deed Federer did for him back in 2001, when they were in
Biel. Federer played the role of driver for Lammer, who'd hurt his
leg. He drove Lammer to school and picked him up from school to
take him to therapy sessions during the treatment period.

Stanislas Wawrinka, another Swiss top tennis player, is also a good friend of Federer's. They have a special bond because they shared good memories of winning gold medals for Switzerland together by playing doubles at the Beijing Olympics in 2008. Federer always loves to see his fellow Swiss players doing well. He offers Wawrinka some advice and support when needed. He was so glad when Wawrinka finally broke through to be ranked in the top ten in 2008. Sometimes it may not be easy for a player to play against a good friend. Federer, however, finds it easier to accept defeat against a good friend. When he lost to Wawrinka in Monte Carlo in 2009, he genuinely felt happy for Wawrinka, saying, 'I'm happy for him that he's progressed so much over the last couple years. He's finally making a push, getting close to top players and beating top players like myself. I think it's great for him … I'm happy for him. Like I told him, the loss doesn't hurt as much just because I know it's against a good guy.' Five years later, in 2014, Wawrinka overtook the Swiss number one spot from Federer by winning his first Grand Slam at the Australian Open. There wasn't any change in their relationship. Federer was extremely happy for Wawrinka's breakthrough. Wawrinka continued to respect Federer and thanked Federer for supporting him throughout his career.

Federer also enjoys popularity among professional women tennis players. They like and admire him for both his talented game and his genial attitude towards them on the tour. Svetlana Kuznetsova, a Russian female player who has won two Grand Slam titles so far in her career, considered Federer special as his piece of nice advice helped her turn around her tennis career. Kuznetsova met Federer at the Beijing Olympics in 2008, when she was urged by her friends to ask Federer to take pictures with them. Federer nicely posed for the pictures and had a ten-minute quality conversation with Kuznetsova. Kuznetsova had lost in the first round in the Olympics and felt she was losing motivation in tennis. She told Federer her problems and her struggle in deciding whether she should move from Spain back to Russia. Federer listened attentively and said to her, 'You can only depend on yourself. You can control it. If you can concentrate and live in Moscow, do this. If you cannot, only you can judge.' This piece of advice backed Kuznetsova's decision to move back to Russia, where she then worked hard and found her passion again. This marked a big turning point in her tennis career. When she won her second Grand Slam in Roland Garros a year later, she revealed to the press how much this special encounter meant to her.

Marion Bartoli was another female player who was amazed by the male champion's kind attention to her. She said, 'I saw him [Federer] after my quarter-final match at the French Open (2011), and he congratulated me for my win and everything. He doesn't have to do it, and he still does it.'

With journalists: The media regards Federer as a pleasant gift. He takes his leadership role as seriously and as smoothly as the media would like it to be. He affirms the role and significance of media in promoting the sports. He has done an excellent job in integrating media into his tennis career. The reporters feel like partners with Federer, whereas they sometimes feel they are being tolerated, if not avoided, by some other players and past champions. Federer has been extraordinary accommodating and generous to the press. He tries his best to fulfil media requests by squeezing them into his packed schedule. For his key victories following mandatory post-match conferences, he often does another couple of hours of individual interviews with loads of reporters.

A revealing example was that after winning the Australian Open in 2006, Federer had done no less than fifteen interviews, lasting until the early hours of the next morning. Even with match losses, Federer does not run away from the press. When he walked off the court after the trophy presentation for one of his toughest losses in the Wimbledon 2008 final, one would think that what he'd most like to do was go straight to the locker room as quickly as he could to settle himself down. On the contrary, he stopped at the NBC Sports microphone, offered a pleasant smile, and answered a couple of questions. He received a big hug from the reporter, John McEnroe, in return.

Federer's proficiency to speak in four languages (Swiss-German, German, English, and French) has made the jobs of the journalists around the world much easier, but not his. In post-match press conferences, he often is interviewed in at least two to three languages, making his interviews always the longest ones among all players. He greets and says hello to reporters when he comes to the conferences. He gives long and thoughtful answers, as if he has hours to prepare them up front. He answers questions politely and patiently, even when the questions are somewhat considered difficult or challenging.

In the interview after Federer's semi-final win over Novak Djokovic in the US Open in 2008, Federer was asked how he would describe his year given that he was in his third straight slam final (after losses in two previous slams) and with the expectations he had of himself and those that everybody had of him. Federer obviously felt it was not the right moment to comment on the year given that his other slam final was due the next day. He responded, 'Let's wait another day and then I will answer that question.' The reporter did not give up and asked, 'How will you describe it if you win at the end of that?' I believe it would be legitimate if Federer did get a bit annoyed by such insistence. However, instead, this amused Federer, and he said with a big smile, 'You can't wait?

Yeah, I don't know. Give me thirty-five hours, and then we'll sit down with something to drink and I'll tell you everything.' The casual and humorous response on the stage brought a round of laughter in the conference room. Federer has always done a decent job in maintaining or restoring a harmonious atmosphere in the press room, even amid some occasional odd moments.

The media perhaps has been so unaccustomed to such a forthcoming champion that nice gestures from Federer are reported repeatedly in their articles. Here are some of those. After Federer won a match that ran until midnight against Lleyton Hewitt in the 2004 Masters Cup, his late night interview got further extended as he, without even a groan, repeated an entire radio interview with a Swiss reporter when the audio equipment failed to record. At Melbourne Park in 2005, when Federer was recording an interview for *Sportsweek*, he tendered his help by walking back and forth along the length of a corridor to check for the best reception.

Federer shows much interest in people who are interested in him. He asks questions about interviewers' jobs and personal lives. Before the 2004 French Open, he visited the editorial department at the *L'Equipe* newspaper in Paris, making reporters grateful enough to praise him in their columns. In 2007, Anjali Rao interviewed him in Hong Kong for CNN Talk Asia. Apart from answering the questions thoughtfully as usual, he practiced on court with Rao and shared tips on making some shots. Federer said he had great fun and thanked Rao for that.

Jonathan Overend from BBC once asked Federer why he spent so much time speaking to the media, and his immediate response was, 'You guys make me laugh.' He was asked the similar question in another interview and he said, 'I see most of you guys practically every day on the tour, so it is no problem for me to spend an hour talking to you, especially if it helps publicise the sport. And anyway, I think some of you are pretty funny!'

With fans: Federer has been awarded the ATP Fans' Favourite Award for a record eleven consecutives years from 2003 to 2013. This shows how popular he has been with fans around the globe. Federer kindly and patiently fulfils fans' requests. He gives enough time to sign autographs, take photos, and show a smile. Even Andy Roddick was impressed by the way the Swiss champion posed for pictures and gave autographs when he hung out with Federer for a couple of days at an exhibition event in 2012. He told the press that he finally understood why people were so fanatical about Federer and why the crowd anywhere cheers for the Swiss.

Federer embraces love from his fans from all over the world. He enjoys cheers and support from fans, and he tries to give back as much as he can. For both victories and losses, he thanks his fans with spontaneous emotions. Off court, he ensures platforms are available for effective communication between him and his fans, including his home page, Facebook, and Twitter. Federer clearly enjoys love from his fans and recognises fans' support as one of his motivators. I think the reciprocal relationship between Federer and fans is highly rewarding for both.

Some incidents caught the media's attention and were reported in several columns to describe the friendly acts of Federer towards fans. After winning the US Open in 2005, when Federer was on his way out of the centre court, he was stopped by some excited kids asking for his autograph. But the kids could not find a pen. Instead of slipping away, the champion waited until a pen was found and then signed the autographs with smiles.

Another incident happened after Federer won his Wimbledon semi-final match against Marat Safin in 2008. He said hello and shook his hand as a few people approached him on his way out of the court. When he almost made an exit, an elderly couple approached; the wife was looking to pose for a photo. He stopped and took the photo kindly, behaving like a well-mannered grandson. A reporter who was on the scene said to Federer, 'You made someone's grandmother very happy.'

During the French Open in 2011, an enthusiastic woman fell to the ground when she tried to squeeze her way over to take a picture of Federer. The woman appeared uninjured but embarrassed. Federer, who was doing an interview with a reporter at the moment, turned casually to walk to the woman, hug her briefly, and pose for a photo. The woman probably felt that her fall made her day.

Sports fans are perhaps already used to receiving thanks from players as part of their victory speech routines. Federer, however, has given fans more. He genuinely shows how much fan support means to him. In his championship speech at the 2006 Australian Open, he said, 'Hundreds and thousands of fans who came out throughout the week, you make it special. Without you, it's not the same.' His voice was shaky as he spoke. The crowds on the stadium looked flattered and tried to give back by bursting into applause as loudly as possible.

Winning the fifth US open in 2008 was especially sweet for Federer, not just because of the history he made for winning five consecutive titles in two different Grand Slam tournaments (Wimbledon and the US Open), but also because it was a big relief after his difficult 2008 season. He felt particularly grateful for continuous support from US fans, despite his below-par season according to his standard and despite generally low favour for non-US players in the States. In his victory speech, he showed his gratitude by saying, 'I love playing the tour. I love playing in front of crowds like you guys. You guys make it worthwhile to practice on a practice court. To make it all the way here is just an incredible feeling for us. I just like to thank you from the bottom of my heart for coming out here for the last couple of weeks. It ... has been incredible for me.'

As a fan, I really wished I were there in the stadiums to seize all these memorable moments. Luckily, Federer obviously was also aware that he had millions of fans around the globe watching his matches on TV. In an effort to show recognition of their support, he always looks for the camera after his matches, smiles nicely, waves to his fans through the camera, and autographs it. I am fully aware of his kind gestures and am delighted every time he makes one. Many other players just autograph the camera mechanically, without showing any sign of appreciation.

During the third-round match of the Miami tournament in 2009, Federer stepped out to the court, waved to the crowd, and walked to his designated seat as usual, only to find that it was raining outside. The umpire decided to postpone the match. Before Federer slowly walked off the court, he smiled to the camera and said, 'See you later.' I almost replied the same thing while at home in front of the TV. It was a warm moment for me.

'I like signing autographs a lot because I think it's something where the players and the fans get together,' Federer said in the press conference after winning the Indian Wells title in 2004. 'They see me from far away, you know, behind. It's just too much space in between us. When they can come close to the players, I think that is a special moment for everybody. If they can take pictures, maybe touch me, whatever, for them it's a highlight of the day. If I can give them that, I think that's a lot of satisfaction for me too.' Apart from being generous to fans, Federer really enjoys those moments he spends with fans. I am happy that over all these years, amid growing demand, Federer has pretty much kept the same positive attitude towards fans. I am happy that I am one of the millions of fans who that Federer has treated as a valuable asset to him.

I believe the above stories are quite revealing themselves. I would like to elaborate a bit here on how an athlete can build positive professional relationships.

- Be approachable: Welcome connections to others. Do not shut yourself down from people around you.
- Be polite: Do not be too lazy or shy to say hello, thanks, or excuse me to others. These are basic positive gestures in interpersonal interactions.
- Show that you care: Care about the welfare of others.
- Show gratitude: Express gratitude to people who have contributed to your professional development and do not hesitate to give back to them in return.
- Show respect: Respect everyone in the profession.
- Be supportive: Be proactive in offering support to others who suffer.
- Pay compliments: Be generous in complimenting others.
- Offer help and advice: Be generous in offering help and advice to others.
- Have a good sense of humour.

Family and couple relationships

Many successful athletes start playing the sports of their lives at very young ages, typically before they are teenagers, so you can imagine how important the role of parents in nurturing their children to be ready for a special and early career in the field of sports. Of course, a family with passion for sports inspires its children's love for sports. Federer's parents played regular club tennis. Messi's entire family consisted of passionate football fans, especially his grandmother, to whom Messi often dedicated his goals by pointing his finger up to the sky after scoring. There are also parents who are directly involved in the sporting careers of their children by taking up professional responsibilities such as coaches, trainers, or agents. What I believe is most important are parents nurturing the personal growth of their children so they become happy and mature athletes. We are going to focus on discussing positive parent-child relationship and positive parenting in raising athletes.

A positive parent-child relationship starts with secure attachment in infancy and early childhood. According to the attachment theory, people who are securely attached in early childhood are more likely as adults to develop secure and trustful adult relationships, including parental, romantic, and social relationships. Secure early childhood attachment means a sensitive and caring physical and emotional bond with at least one primary caregiver. On the contrary, an insecure attachment during early childhood impairs development of one's capacity to love and develop stable relationships, as there is so much mistrust and anxiety involved during the critical period of shaping their beliefs about people and the world. Therefore, parents who want to grow a loving capacity and sense of interpersonal security in their children must provide them with secure and sensitive bonding starting in infancy. Professional development of an athlete starts very early. It demands a great deal of courage for children to take on a completely different path from their friends or schoolmates. Therefore, trustful relationships are necessary to back them up.

Parents are definitely the earliest role models for children. When watching tennis matches, I like to look at reactions from players' parents and relatives in the players' boxes. We can learn something about their characters and look for traces of effects on the players' on-court and off-court manners. For example, Toni Nadal, Nadal's uncle and coach, has been rather vocal in the player's box. A few times, the umpire had to give Nadal warnings about his on-court coaching. Toni has been a lifetime coach for Nadal and obviously is a very hands-on coach. Nadal's dependence on Toni is therefore a natural result. Often we could also see Toni clapping his hands hard when he saw excellent ball striking, even from Nadal's opponents. Toni's sole appreciation of excellence in tennis has helped push Nadal for continuous improvement year after year.

It's not that rare to hear players complaining about being disturbed by the loudness coming from the opponent's player box. For example, Djokovic's player box is often quite packed and very energised. Cheers coming from the box can be quite over the line and arouse complaints from time to time. How about Federer's entourage? They cheer for Federer with mediocre intensity and calmness. They never get too loud or annoying. They show fine support to Federer and respect for the other player on the court. When thrilled Nadal ran over to hug his team after his epic win over Federer at Wimbledon in 2008, the camera caught a scene that I found quite revealing. Nadal ran past Federer's dad on his way to reach his team. From what I saw, his dad, without a trace of loathing, watched Nadal kindly with a smile on his face, his hands busy clapping. I guess we can get a good idea of how Federer has been positively influenced by his parents, perhaps genetically and through positive parenting as well. Federer's parents, Lynette

Federer and Robert Federer, are described as liberal, nice, and modest people. They have been good role models for Federer.

There are four basic styles of parenting, categorised by the dimensions of demand and responsiveness: (1) Neglectful parenting means the parent is neither demanding nor responsive. The parents with this style are usually uninvolved, detached, and dismissive with their children. 2) Parent with indulgent parenting is responsive but not demanding. Such permissive and non-directive parenting may create a spoiled child. 3) Authoritarian parent is demanding but not responsive. The parenting is restrictive and punitive with little communication because it is mainly about conformity and compliance from the child. 4) Parents with authoritative parenting are both demanding and responsive. Authoritative parenting encourages children to be independent but still places limits and controls on their actions. Mr and Mrs Federer's authoritative style of parenting helped Federer to grow into a good-natured and responsible individual. They were attentive and responsive to the needs of Federer, but at the same time, they set standards and limits for his behaviour. They helped Federer to self-explore and develop autonomy himself.

At the age of fourteen, Federer made a big decision to move alone to the Swiss national tennis centre in Ecublens to pursue a better tennis training opportunity. Given the closeness of the family, this was a significant change, not only to Federer but also to the family. Lynette recalled the moment[14] 'We are a close family, but Roger took the decision at a very early age that he wanted to play tennis away from home. His father and I saw our role as supporting his project, to help him develop his own confidence, and to help him if things didn't turn out quite the way he would have wished. We never forced him to do anything; we let him develop on his own. He made a lot of important decisions himself when he was young, and that was key to his success. He learnt to be very independent.'

Federer's parents, of course, always have strong belief in their son's talent, but they never held their expectations up too high and forced their son to get there. The mother of the hosting family in Ecublens, Cornelia Christinet, said she learnt much from the Federer couple. She credited the couple for not being overprotective, and they were tolerant and understanding when things did not work out for Federer during his period in Ecublens.[15] The couple dealt with Federer's teenage mistakes with wisdom and sensitivity. Lynette told the media a story of her son's insensitivity towards a new Turkish girl classmate in primary school.[16] The Turkish girl was given more attention from teachers since she could not speak German, and that aroused complaints from Federer and his other classmates about unfair treatment. Instead of scolding, she guided Federer to put himself in the girl's shoes, to imagine how he'd feel alone among strangers who didn't understand him and who didn't have the kindness to help him adjust. Federer's teacher also began teaching the class about Turkey and had Federer and his classmates learn to speak Turkish. 'Just learning to count to ten was very hard,' Federer recalled. 'When that happened to me, I finally understood what the girl must have felt. This could be a very good lesson for children to learn how to grow empathy and acceptance.'

Contrasting his composure on the professional tour, Federer was known for his teenage temper on court. His tantrums were pointed more towards himself than towards opponents, umpires, or anyone else. He took his tennis setbacks very hard and had difficulty accepting defeat in his early days. He commented on every shot and yelled, with a lot of throwing rackets. His parents understood that his tantrums came from his own expectations about his game, which he cared a lot about. They tried to put forth perspectives of how tantrum could adversely affect his tennis and why he needed to pull himself together in setbacks for the goodness of his tennis. On the one hand, they showed understanding. On the other hand, they stayed firm and told Federer how his bad behaviour on court upset them.

On one occasion, Federer's parents called out to try to quiet Federer down in a match, but Federer shouted back, 'Go and have a drink and leave me alone.' Then they drove Federer home quietly, sending him signals about his misbehaviour. 'Roger never heard a bad word from us just because he had lost, but when he misbehaved or when he just didn't make an effort, we weren't going to let that go,' Lynette said in an interview with the *Basler Zeitung*.[15] 'He always had to take responsibility for the consequences. If he dug himself into a hole, he had to dig himself out of it,' Lynette added.

It is never easy to keep harmony intact in a family with a gifted child since much of the focus and resources are inevitably directed towards that particular child. However, the Federer family stayed relatively harmonious. Diana Federer, Federer's older sister, managed to stay away from the limelight shed from the tennis world. She grew to be an independent individual, with a career as a psychiatric nurse and her life away from tennis. I think the parents did a great job in nurturing a gifted child without upsetting the normal functioning of a family.

Mr and Mrs Federer have always been supportive of Federer's tennis career. They essentially changed their lives and schedules to some extent to accommodate Federer's career pursuit. They watched Federer play at important matches. They have been significant members of Federer's team, but they let Federer lead his own team. 'I view myself as working in an advisory capacity and trying to disburden Roger whenever possible,' Robert said. Lynette helps by answering Federer's fan mail. Apart from that, Lynette's main responsibility is to help run the Roger Federer Foundation, which was established in December 2003. 'When Roger was starting to earn good money, his father and I said, "We think it's a good thing you give back a bit of your own fortune to those who are less advantaged,"' Lynette said.

His parents also added value to Federer's work ethic. 'My parents would always ask me to ensure that I didn't waste their money when I was using practice courts or getting coaching as a kid,' Federer told *Daily Mail* in an interview that took place in 2010.[17] 'They always said that they didn't mind driving me around Switzerland every weekend to play in a tournament, just as long as I put in a good effort and a decent performance … They were fine whether I won or lost, as long as I tried hard and didn't waste their weekends.'

So what have we learned? To raise a child to become both a positive person and a respectable sportsman, the parent-child relationship has to be secure, trustful, and supportive in the first place. Parents should allow room for their children to explore their interests in sports rather than imposing one on them. Parents may believe they know what's best for their children because of their well-established knowledge and life experiences. However, they need to allow their children to enjoy certain autonomy so that the children can learn a sense of responsibility. For teenagers who decide to dedicate themselves to sports, they need to feel that they want it more than anybody else, not just fulfilling the wishes of others. Positive parenting emphasises growing self-esteem and optimism in children. Only parents who have strong belief in their children can do it. Finally, parents have to be children's positive role models in developing the right attitudes for pursuing happy and successful lives.

Having good parents equals a happy childhood. Having a good marriage equals a happy adulthood. Of course, it is not that straightforward and simple. But for a grown-up couple relationship, or marriage, it has been proved a crucial factor in determining one's well-being. A satisfying couple relationship is loving, communicative, and mutually supportive. It helps carry us safely through the difficulties in our lives. It also gives us strength to pursue things we want for our lives. It is exactly what is needed for becoming a great athlete. Pursuing success in sports requires many sacrifices. For some physically demanding sports, the injuries and pain that athletes are bearing can be rather upsetting. For some sports, like tennis, the players have to travel to all over the world year after year to sustain their careers.

Many sports demand a stringent life routine concerning diet, rest, sleep, and even leisure activity. Athletes have often been asked to give up their favourite meals, hobbies, and some personal habits. That does not just affect the athletes but their close partners. So having an understanding partner is very important to an athlete's striving for success. Stability in a couple relationship is positively correlated with consistency in performance. As revealed in Andre Agassi's autobiography, *Open*[18], a happy marriage with Steffi Graf, one of the most successful women tennis players, apparently saved him from the disappointing low of his career and his lousy life at that point.

Any theory or principle developed for enhancing couple relationship revolves around a basic ingredient: *love*. Love is about reciprocal sharing of care and acceptance. It involves affection, passion, intimacy, and commitment. In a loving relationship, we value each other's well-being and turn to each other for support and affirmation when in need. Loving is an inborn survival ability. Everyone has the capacity to love and be loved. However, such a loving capacity varies and can grow or diminish with life experiences. We therefore have to keep nurturing it throughout our lives.

Federer has openly shared many times that having a stable and loving relationship with Miroslava Vavrinec (Mirka), now his wife, has contributed much to his career success. The sweet couple began their relationship in 2000, when they met and played tennis for Switzerland in the Sydney Olympics. About a year later, Mirka retired from her tennis career due to a foot injury. Mirka once revealed how she got through her dark period. 'Roger was my greatest support back then. He gave my tennis life back to me. When he wins, it's as if I win as well.' She then took up the role of a personal assistant for Federer, dealing with media requests and Federer's schedule. Since then, Mirka has accompanied Federer in his travels all over the world, going to almost every tournament Federer played in over all the years.

To Federer, Mirka is not just a lover but also a practice partner, a colleague, a companion, and a soul mate. In an interview by *Daily Mail* in 2007[19], Federer revealed how Mirka carried herself as the woman supporting him and his career. 'When we met, I wasn't famous and probably ranked number fifty at best. Mirka was making her own career, but after she was injured and couldn't play anymore, I asked her if she wanted to help me. It was a difficult time for her. But this way she had the chance to travel, to be with me every day, and I think this made her happy again. We soon realised we really loved each other and we liked hanging out together. She still loves the sport of tennis, the competitive edge it offers. Maybe, in a way, her own career goes on with me. She feels she is needed for me to be successful. She loves what she does.' There has been intense closeness and commitment between these two lovely persons. 'Instead of pulling me away from tennis, she pushes me towards it. She likes being involved, but in the end, she's my girlfriend, and that's what's most important,' Federer added.

Federer does not tour with a big group of people. Mirka's accompanying him has apparently been a key source of comfort to him during his demanding tour schedule. 'One of the most important things is to wake up in the morning and see her next to me in bed. It's a very special feeling, knowing she's there. She takes care of me and does what's best for me,' Federer told the Spanish news service EPE in 2007.[20] When Federer was asked what Mirka meant to him in an interview by *Deutsche Presse-Agentur, DPA*[21] in the same year, he said, 'She is the most important person in my life, of course, with my parents. And I am very glad about everything she does for me. She will remain my girlfriend or my wife, and she does everything that she does only because she has fun helping me.'

Mirka's affirmation contributes much to Federer's self-confidence. Federer told the press in 2006 that he did not often get a chance to reflect on what he had achieved, and therefore positive feedback from Mirka helped in this aspect. 'That is the nicest moment for me, when Mirka tells me that she is proud that I can handle it all. Those are the times, when I'm talking to Mirka, when I feel really good about myself,' Federer said. Federer does try to give back to Mirka as much as he can. He gives Mirka his time during off season, doing things Mirka wants to do. 'If she wants to go shopping for ten hours, I go with her, because she has to wait for me for ten hours in every tournament. I have no problem with that.' Federer was willing to put Mirka as the centre of attention during vacation.

Federer married Mirka on 11th April 2009 in his home town of Basel. It was a private wedding, surrounded by a small group of close friends and family. Federer talked about his wedding later in a pre-match interview in Monte Carlo: 'It was nice sharing the moment with my family, my closest friends. I got very emotional, yet again. So it was very nice. It was just nice to know that *she loves me so much and I love her so much*.' During the Roland Garros tournament in 2009, Mirka was pregnant and still watched every match of Federer's. Federer said, 'She was with me day in and day out, throughout the world, and she helped me considerably, as a person. I developed faster, grew faster with her. Thanks to her, I was very calm in the important moments in my career. She was always here, always supportive. I owe her a lot.' These are probably the nicest and most beautiful words I have ever heard in expressing one's love and thankfulness for another.

After Federer's lovely twins were born, family attention naturally shifted to the twins. Federer, however, did not de-emphasise his role as a husband. 'I think we love being fathers of kids. And being a husband is for me as big a priority as being a father,' Federer said. 'Knowing what she would do for me, knowing what she would do for them [the twins], is very emotional.'[4]

LZ Granderson of ESPN recalled his first interview with Federer. When he asked Federer what he loved, he was expecting answers like movies, chocolate, or winning. Instead, Federer gave him a name and said, 'I love Mirka.'

On the one hand, Mirka can't be more supportive of Federer's tennis career. On the other hand, Federer can't be more grateful to have such a great partner. The relationship of this lovely couple demonstrates several important components in building a loving relationship (not limited to couple relationships, though):

- *Sharing*: We should openly share our resources, feelings, and opinions with someone we love.

- *Caring*: We should care about the needs of someone we love and try our best to help fulfil that person's needs.
- *Commitment*: We should be loyal to someone we love and readily carry out all obligations that go with the relationships.
- *Trust*: We should trust people we love, having faith in them.
- *Sensitivity*: We should be aware of and responsive to the feelings and needs of others.
- *Support*: When others seek our support, we give them time, patience, and encouragement.

If we nurture these components as much as possible in our relationships, we can grow our love and thereby enhance our relationships. Finally, we have to clear ourselves of any self-defeating beliefs, such as 'I do not deserve to be loved', 'I am not worthy of any love', and so forth. One should enjoy reciprocal love from others and believe that everyone deserves to be loved. We have to readily accept others' caring and concern, also seeking support from others when we are in need.

Socialising

Social interaction is an important source of happiness. A good social network can fulfil one's need for help, companionship, support, and recognition. Athletes, with their strong physiques, usually present images of being tough and hard. People may forget about softer sides of them. They need to hang around with friends to relax and have fun. They sometimes need consolation from friends to soothe their defeated spirits. There are certain myths about those famous athletes. For instances, they only make friends with people with big names and similar statuses. Little effort is needed for them to make friends, as other people should feel honoured to take all the initiative in getting close to them. No. They have normal friends too. Just like everybody else, they have to invest time and effort in making and keeping friends.

'When I'm home, I try to catch up with everybody. I don't want to become a stranger to my friends,' Federer said when asked about how he spent his days off tour. Clearly, friendships matter to Federer. He has to make a conscious effort to keep connected with his old friends because he spends so much time away from home. He enjoys making new friends on tour too. He has always been an easy-going and socialising individual who enjoys interacting with people. This definitely has made his life much easier and happier, as a tennis career involves many interactions with officials, media, and fans.

His good comprehension of different languages also represents an edge for him to connect with people from all over the world. A *New York Times* article in 2007 highlighted Federer's fondness for linking with others. The author considered the use of headphones as a convenient way to hide from the public, tuning out autograph requests or questions. Federer refused to do so with his iPod and said, 'I think they're a great creation, but if you put them on, you can't speak to anyone. You're isolating yourself, and I don't like that.'[22]

Federer is good at developing immediate rapport with people. Chris Bowers, a freelance writer for the tennis circuit, first interviewed Federer when Federer won his Wimbledon Junior title. In his book, *Roger Federer: Spirit of a Champion,* he described his first impression of Federer: 'He made instant connections with people. He certainly made me feel he was pleased to have chatted with me'.[14]

Canadian doubles specialist Daniel Nestor, who has been on the tennis field for a few generations, described Federer's connectivity with people in these words: 'He jokes around with everyone, knows everyone's name, says hi to everyone, and has time for everybody, which is the most important thing.' Federer cares much about how other players are doing on the tour. He is usually one of those, if not the first, to send messages to show concern and support when his fellow players are injured. He pays attention to how lower-ranked players play in smaller tournaments. John Isner arrived at the Australian Open in 2010 after claiming his first title in Auckland's Heineken Open, a lower tier tournament, the week before. A congratulatory greeting from Federer in the player's cafe surprised him. 'That was pretty cool. I didn't really think he would even know (about his win), but he did. Any time Roger can talk to you, let alone congratulate you, it's pretty neat,' Isner told the press.

Some of Federer's closest friends now are his old buddies who've been friends with him since he was a child. One of them is Marco Chiudinelli. Their friendship started back at their training days in a tennis club in Basel when they were eight years old. Talking about Federer as a friend, Chiudinelli said, 'You could always rely on him, talk with him, and count on him.'

Yves Allegro was Federer's roommate back in his teens. They became good friends and later double partners in the professional tour. Allegro enjoyed playing doubles with Federer despite the fact that the double game had naturally become less of a priority to Federer. Chiudinelli and Allegro, who are still active tennis players, remain Federer's closest friends. Even though they have much lower rankings and play sometimes only in the qualifying rounds, Federer still keeps a close eye on their matches and gives them support and cheer when needed.

Even in a very competitive environment, friendship can shine and give a touch of warmth. In the first round of Wimbledon in 2008, a friendly changeover took place and surprised the spectators at Centre Court, which was supposed to be at a time of heat and fight. When Dominik Hrbaty, Federer's old doubles partner, was down two sets and 2–5 in the third set against Federer, he walked away from his designated side and sat next to Federer during the changeover. They chatted for a minute just like friends having a lazy happy hour gathering. The crowd clearly appreciated the sweet moment and responded with giggles and claps. When Federer served for the match, one guy in the crowd even shouted, 'Give him a chance, Roger.' Federer patiently paused his serving and nicely invited a round of applause for Hrbaty from the crowd. Federer later said he appreciated Hrbaty's friendly move and enjoyed sharing with him such an unusual moment on Centre Court. He later disclosed their private chat. 'I said to Dominik, "Well, I'm very happy that you appreciate playing against me." He said that it was a match that was a great honour for him to actually not only play against me but [also to] be my friend. I said to him, "Well, same for me …"'

On 7 June 2009, when Federer had his best chance ever to win his first French Open Slam in the final against Robin Soderling, the tennis crowd at Roland Garros was obviously excited to cheer for Federer and witness history being made. In a nearby country, a group of fellow players, including James Blake, were watching the match on TV in the players' lounge at the Aegon Championships, a grass court tournament before Wimbledon, in London. It was obvious whom they were rooting for. 'We wanted to see Roger make history,' Blake said. The support Federer received could be justified, to a certain extent, by fellow players' appreciation of greatness and tennis history. It also reflected how affable Federer was to his fellow players.

Federer and Nadal, being the rivalry at the top of the game for a very long time, never show any sign of resentment against each other. They have a friendship that is atypically harmonious and respectful. Federer talked to CNN in 2009 about his friendship with Nadal: 'Rafa is not only a wonderful player but a real nice guy too. We sit on the Player Council board together. I am the president, and he is the vice-president, and we discuss what is good for the image of the game. We both realise the position and role we play within our sport, and we both want to show that you can have a rivalry without it becoming aggressive. When we go on court, we want to beat each other, but when we come off the court, we are friends again.'[23] Federer believed that competition with Nadal made both of them better players and forged a stronger bonding of friendship between them. Nadal shared pretty much the same view with Federer on their friendship. Cultivating friendships on the tour definitely made the tour more enjoyable for Federer and made him a happier tennis player.

To media and fans, Federer's friendships with Tiger Woods and Pete Sampras drew much attention and interest. Federer took the initiative to link up with these two sports legends, and the friendships have proven to be inspirational to him. Sampras has always been a rather quiet and cool champion in the tennis field. All the other players in his era respected him, but very few could come close to him on personal terms. So it is a particularly nice story for the two tennis greats, who were both so dominant in their respective eras, to have built a friendship even though they only played each other once on the professional tour. Sampras text messaged Federer during the US Open in 2006 and called to congratulate Federer in person after his victory. Fedcrer was clearly flattered. They've exchanged text messages on a regular basis since then. Federer brought the relationship closer by practicing with Sampras on several occasions and engaging in more in-depth communication in some exhibition matches in Asia. The commonalities and mutual understanding between them helped consolidating Federer's perspectives about the game.

Sampras has never been shy of showing his appreciation about Federer and has praised his special friend openly and consistently despite the fact that they are in fact competing against each other for tennis records. Federer shows a great deal of respect towards Sampras as a tennis legend who has contributed so much to the history of the game. Sampras is not active in public now and most of the time prefers to be at home parenting his children. However, he flew a long way to London to watch Federer win his fifteenth Grand Slam and witness his own record being broken. Federer, of course, felt extra happy and grateful to have the right man there sharing his historic moment.

Long before Federer got to know Tiger Woods in person, media had already been comparing the achievement, champion spirit, and character of the two because they shared similar legendary status in their respective sports. When Federer and Woods were asked about their views about each other, they expressed forthright admiration. Finally, in 2006, Federer came up with the idea of meeting Woods in person. The result of the invitation, arranged by his agent, was that Woods would like to see Federer play in the US Open final. At that time, the tournament had not even started yet, so it added a little more pressure on Federer to come through to the final. He did get the job done eventually. In the final, he had Woods and Woods's wife sitting in his guest box rooting for him. The moment was great for Federer, though he had to bear additional pressure to level up his game to impress his honourable guest.

After Federer won the championship, Federer and Woods celebrated together, chatting and taking pictures with the trophy. Since then, they have been friends. They talked and sent messages to each other. Given their dominance in their sports, they had an understanding of what it takes for them to be up there. They share similar visions, mindsets, and approaches in their sports. That was where their friendship clicked in. They supported and encouraged each other.

Woods said, 'Our text messages are pretty funny. We do needle each other pretty good. But [there is] also a lot of support. He's one of the first ones to always congratulate me, and vice versa. Wherever I'm playing in the world, he's always following what I'm doing and I'm following what he's doing.' Woods woke up early at home to watch Federer complete his career Grand Slam at Roland Garros. He said he even yelled at the TV when Federer went through some tough moments during the match. Unfortunately, Woods's image as a role model fell apart due to the scandal about his marital infidelity in 2009. Federer could not do much to help, but he gave his friend sympathy, support, and best wishes.

Humour is definitely a catalyst for social interactions. Humorous and playful people laugh a lot and are good at making others laugh too. They love their own jokes and can joke comfortably in front of people. They do not mind making fun of themselves or being subjects of other people's jokes. They are good at maintaining a delighted atmosphere, even in some tough moments. My Swiss idol does make me laugh quite often. That is part of the reason I like him so much; I personally like to laugh and value humour a lot. On court, Federer plays and fights with decent composure. Off court, his composure is not too difficult to be cracked. A little joke can send him way off. I have seen dozens of videos where he broke into unstoppable giggles doing such things as interviews and filming commercials. I think Federer is such an inborn lover of laughter that sometimes it takes virtually nothing to set him off. It is so much fun watching those videos, and I have watched them many times. Crazy me.

Tony Roche, who was Federer's coach, was also fond of Federer's character. Roche once explained what made him get along well with Federer[24] 'He's good fun. He enjoys a bit of a laugh [and is] very relaxed, and that's a big part of why he's so successful.' Pete Sampras once said, 'Roger is such a great guy, and we had a lot of laughs over dinners. He is a funny guy, he likes his jokes, and he is a bit of a prankster.'[25] Federer's interviews may not be as hilarious as Roddick's, but dropping a few lines of humorous comments from grinning Federer are actually quite common. To me, humour definitely is part of Federer's great charisma, though it may not be shown as often or be as demonstrative as his elegance in tennis.

In conclusion, to build positive social networks, we need to spend enough time socialising in order to cultivate empathy and a sense of humour in ourselves as well as improve our social skills.

1) Spend time socialising

- Spend enough time on social activities.
- Catch up with old buddies from time to time to replenish friendships.

- Do not reject invitations automatically due to a busy schedule. Try to figure out your timetable in order to accommodate social activities.
- Take chances and initiatives to make new friends.

2) Cultivate empathy. (Empathy is the emotion that connects people. To empathise means to share and to experience the feelings of another person. When one feels empathy for other people in need or in pain, one experiences the urge to show concern and help. Empathy is not something that can be learned overnight.)

- Learn more about emotions.
- Increase insight to your own emotions.
- Open yourself to experience emotions of others.
- Remind yourself to stay warm-hearted.

3) Improve your sense of humour.

- Smile and laugh as much as you can.
- Listen to jokes; read funny books; watch comedies.
- Share your funny and interesting experiences with others.
- Surround yourself with cheerful and playful people.

4) Improve your social skills

- Listening: to listen sincerely to what other people say
- Affirmation: to show appropriate appreciation to others

- Sharing: to enhance sharing in a social group
- Conflict resolution: to learn to compromise with others in disagreements

It is undeniable that building positive relationships is a natural desire in most of us, from the first moment we seek positive attachments with our parents as babies. As we grow, we need more – maybe loving partners, good buddies, or nice co-workers – in order to feel as if we are living a fulfilled life. Overall, we have to remember three pathways to boost this particular element of well-being:

1) Find positives in your current relationships: Discarding dissatisfactory relationships is sometimes not easy and in some cases not probable. Our lives, therefore, can become stuck if we pile up negative bias towards our current relationships. Learn to appreciate more the positive aspects of people surrounding you – their good personalities, good behaviours, and good intentions.

2) Choose and engage yourself in positive relationships: Beware that in many circumstances, we do have the choice in choosing our relationships, even though the choices may not be as explicit or abundant as we may wish. Remind yourself to make conscious choices to engage yourself in relationships that are more encouraging, inspiring, and accommodating.

3) Exert positive influence on your relationships: In a more proactive way, you may try to influence people around you to become more positive – for example, fostering some positive perspectives, sharing happy and interesting

experiences, arranging enjoyable social gatherings, creating friendly and communicative atmospheres, and so forth. Spend time and effort building mutually rewarding relationships.

CHAPTER 5

Meaning (M)

Meaning has both a subjective and objective component. On the one hand, meaning can be unique and personal. When people feel so positive about doing certain things that they believe are significant to themselves and others, they think that what they are doing is meaningful. On the other hand, meaning has an objective component that complies with certain universal principles about humanity and moral standards. People who help alleviate the sufferings of humankind may feel miserable, but their work is likely to be seen as meaningful. Meaning is often pursued for its own sake and definitely contributes much to one's well-being. As proposed by Dr. Martin Seligman, sense of meaning is found when we feel we are belonging to and serving something that is bigger than our individual selves. A meaningful life is achieved by utilising our signature strengths and virtues in the service of something much larger than we are. Meaning guides our choices and actions consciously and subconsciously. Knowing what makes our lives meaningful give us a sense of life direction. We need to make sense of our own experiences in order to cultivate our sense of self-worth and self-identity.

Utilisation of signature strengths

Virtues are characteristics we value as promoting individual and collective well-being of society. Virtues are positive by nature. Dr. Seligman and his team have drawn from major religious and philosophical traditions six core human virtues that have been more commonly endorsed: wisdom, courage, humanity, justice, temperance and transcendence (as shown in the table below).[1] They further identified and formulated distinct routes to each of the six virtues. These distinct routes are called character strengths, which are good, measurable, and acquirable qualities of people that may guide us in pursuing the virtues. Character strengths are largely trait-like (i.e., characteristics that people demonstrate across situations and over time). These strengths, although considered dispositional qualities with stability and generality, can be built or improved with enough effort and determination. It is our choice whether to develop and use the strengths in our daily lives.

List of six virtues and twenty-four character strengths

Virtues	Character Strengths
I. Wisdom and knowledge (Qualities in acquisition and use of knowledge)	1. Curiosity/interest in the world 2. Love of learning 3. Judgement/critical thing/ open-mindedness 4. Ingenuity/originality/ practical intelligence 5. Social intelligence/personal intelligence/emotional intelligence 6. Perspective

II. Courage (Qualities of willpower to accomplish goals amid challenge)	7. Valour and bravery 8. Perseverance/industry/diligence 9. Integrity/genuineness/honesty
III. Humanity and love (Qualities that enable friendly, caring, and loving relationships)	10. Kindness and generosity 11. Loving and allowing oneself to be loved
IV. Justice (Qualities that promote equity in social groups or community)	12. Citizenship/duty/teamwork/loyalty 13. Fairness and equity 14. Leadership
V. Temperance (Qualities that involves self-regulation for goodness)	15. Self-control 16. Prudence/discretion/caution 17. Humility and modesty
VI. Transcendence (Qualities that bring broader connections and meaning to life)	18. Appreciation of beauty and excellence 19. Gratitude 20. Optimism/hope 21. Spirituality/sense of purpose/faith/religiousness 22. Forgiveness and mercy 23. Playfulness and humour 24. Vitality (zest/passion/enthusiasm)

Signature strengths are the most signifying character strengths of a person. According to Dr. Seligman, signature strengths have the following characteristics:

- A sense of ownership and authenticity
- A feeling of excitement while displaying it, particularly at first
- A rapid learning curve as themes are attached to the strength
- Continuous learning of new ways to enact the strength
- A sense of yearning to act in accordance with the strength
- A feeling of inevitability in using the strength
- Invigoration rather than exhaustion when using the strength
- The creation and pursuit of fundamental projects that revolve around the strength
- Intrinsic motivation to use the strength
- Feeling of joy and enthusiasm while using it

It is believed that using our signature strengths in the main realms of our lives can bring abundant gratification and authentic happiness. When we further extend our utilization of signature strengths to areas that go beyond ourselves, we take our experiences to another level: the pursuit of a meaningful life.

Fostering sportsmanship

In the world of sports, despite the fact that individual sport achievement attracts a great deal of attention, certainly other qualities go beyond it and are more highly valued. Sportsmanship no doubt stands out above all as the highest spirit in the field.

Sportsmanship guides how a sportsman should behave generally in sports activities. It represents virtues such as fairness, integrity, respect, and persistence. Real sports lovers always want a game to be played fairly. We like to see athletes paying respect to their opponents and other people involved in the sport. A good manner is expected in both winning and losing situations. Winners who gloat about their wins and belittle their opponents are bad winners. Losers who make excuses and blame others for their defeats are sore losers. Neither a bad winner nor a sore loser exhibits good sportsmanship. Whether winning or losing, sportsmanship demands athletes to compete wholeheartedly and decisively until the end – no quitting and no tanking.

A flourished sportsman should therefore endeavour to exhibit sportsmanship and aspire to foster sportsmanship in the industry. Roger Federer not only elevated the game to another level; he also elevated the game's standard of sportsmanship. He has won the ATP World Tour's Stefan Edberg Sportsmanship Award for a record nine times (from 2004–2009 and from 2011–2013). The award is the most telling recognition for equity and fairness in men's tennis. The award is voted by fellow players every year for a player who, throughout the year, conducted himself at the highest level of professionalism and integrity, who competed with his fellow players with the utmost spirit of fairness.

Federer was given the award during his prime years, when the other players looked upon him as the field leader and role model. In 2010, the award went to Rafael Nadal, who was also highly regarded for his sportsmanship. The years 2011 and 2013 were Federer's slimmest in terms of titles won. He was still given the honour those two years. I believed this reflected how other players admired Federer for remaining fair and earnest amid his down times. The only player who won the award five times (over eight years) was Stefan Edberg. The award was named after him. But perhaps the award should eventually be renamed the Roger Federer Sportsmanship Award. Federer was also awarded the Prix Orange five consecutive times from 2005–2009. The Prix Orange prize was awarded to the ambassador of sportsmanship, as voted by the French public and press online.

In the following paragraphs, I will highlight the character strengths that characterise sportsmanship:

Fairness and equity: Fairness and equity are results of moral judgement that emphasise treating people equally and with justice. A person with this character strength values fair chances and tries to apply the same principles to everyone. This strength applies not only to a competitive environment where people are fighting for resources and rewards, but also to social relationships where people attain harmony by being fair to each other. Fairness and equity are the most essential qualities for sportsmanship. For every single sport, certain explicit and implicit rules bind the participants in order to constitute a fair game. Attractiveness of sports relies very much on having athletes competing on the same ground with fair chances. So as athletes, it would mean much to them if they could exhibit these aspects of sportsmanship and earn respect from others as a result.

Federer has been very outspoken about issues regarding fairness of the game. To ensure fair games in men's tennis, Federer supports rigorous drug testing to keep the sport clean. Back in 2004, Federer said before the Dubai Open, 'It's not a problem being tested all the time.' (He took twenty-one drug tests in 2003, the most among the players.) 'Obviously, after a loss, you're not quite in the mood to go and do a test, but I understand it. Testing has been done very aggressively, I would say, in a good way, because it is something which is important to me – that the sport of tennis stays clean.' In 2009, a more stringent drug-testing regime was imposed, and it raised strong oppositions from many top players, including Rafael Nadal and Andy Murray. The new system was criticised for being too intrusive. Federer, too, did not like it, but acknowledged its importance to the integrity of tennis. 'I know it's a pain, but I would like it to be a clean sport, and that's why I'm OK with it,' Federer said. Again, Federer placed fairness and cleanness of the tennis game above his own preference. Federer was concerned or even scared by the match-fixing issues that happened in tennis in 2007. He found gambling on one's own sport totally unacceptable, as it jeopardised the cleanness of tennis, which he always wanted to protect.

Despite Federer's generally likable personality and aptitude of not making too controversial statements, there were times that Federer did upset other players and have rounds of arguments back and forth. He greatly appreciates when his opponents play the game fairly but gets irritated when his opponents play tricks or abuse the rules. He became quite vocal when he felt the fairness of the game was offended. One of the controversial issues perhaps was about the use of injury breaks. For a certain period, Federer was clearly annoyed by the abusive use of injury breaks by some players. When he believed the fairness of the game was jeopardised in the match, he showed no hesitation in voicing his concern. During the play-off round for the Davis Cup world group in 2007, Switzerland was drawn against Serbia. Novak Djokovic, a Serbian tennis player, called for a trainer to massage his leg when he went two sets to one down against Stanislas Wawrinka, Federer's teammate. At that time, Djokovic had a reputation of tactical use of injury breaks. When Federer was asked about this, he said, 'I think he's a joke when it comes to his injuries. The rules are there to be used but not abused.' Given his clear stance on the use of these breaks, Federer later said he was happy that players seldom played the tricks again in his matches. Even when Federer took a legitimate injury break, which was very rare, he felt sorry about it, as he believes it is a bit unfair to interrupt his opponent's play. He even apologised to his opponents for calling injury breaks, whereas we seldom saw other players doing so.

It is not only fairness during matches that matters; Federer tries to ensure fair commentary. For example, he believes it is not fair to take credit away from players who make great efforts to beat him. He once said after he lost his match, 'Never take anything away from somebody who beat me, because I was trying my best.' During the pre–French Open clay court season in 2010, Federer answered the routine question about his chance of winning the French. Despite being the defending champion, he declined to claim himself the favourite and said he would rather give the honour to his rival, Nadal. 'He [Nadal] has been on an absolute tear for the last five years,' Federer said. 'He's hardly lost any matches – you can almost count those on one hand – and he's only lost one match at the French Open, so I would think he's still the favourite. I would love to say I'm the big favourite, but I don't think it's quite right, even though I won the French Open last year.' If you read into his lines, it was clearly not a case of false modestly but an unbiased comment from Federer.

Being a representative of the sport for a long period, Federer, more than any player on the tour, understands and respects the interests of various tennis parties, including top players, lower ranked players, tennis organizations, sponsors, and fans. When prompted to give an opinion on controversial issues, Federer tries to go beyond his self-interest, be fair to different parties, and consider the benefits of the sport as a whole. His fellow players trust him because he is a fair and selfless leader. Many lesser known players have openly credited Federer for considering the interests of them rather than focusing on fulfilling interests of the top players.

Around the end of 2011 season, the field was heated up by strong protests from some top players against the long and packed tour schedule. Andy Murray was the most outspoken player on the issue and even threatened to have a strike among players. While the tough and demanding tennis season earned players some sympathy, Murray's strike threat aroused criticisms that unfortunately caused some damage to the image of tennis. During periods of difficult economic environments, where many people worried about losing their jobs, groaning from a tennis player who was earning huge prize money obviously did not sound good at all. Federer remained relatively silent until he was asked for an opinion during the World Tour Final in London. He agreed that the tour was long and demanding, but he saw no reason for any boycott action, especially when the season next year would already be shortened by two weeks after long-term negotiations with the officials. He understood that shortening the tour would mean killing some tournaments, whereas many people's work were involved. In addition, he knew that some lower ranked players actually welcomed more tournaments and longer seasons for them to make their living and accumulate ranking points.

Having been on the top level for so long, Federer still does not forget how players struggle at second- or third-tier levels, and thus he was concerned about their fair chance. He also gave his opinion on the suggestion of a two-year ranking system instead of one year. 'I think it's not a good thing for the lower-ranked players, to be quite honest. I think it's going to be a struggle for them to make a big breakthrough,' Federer said. 'I know it could be a good thing for me or for Rafa or for other good players because we would stay at the top for a very long time. For us to move down in the rankings would take something extraordinary. But for the lower-ranked players, I don't think it's a good thing, and that's why I can't support it.' In answering questions from the press during the London Olympic in 2012, Federer expressed his concern about having ranking points for the Olympics. He said it was not fair for some of the players who were not eligible to play the Olympic tournament, as only four players per country were allowed to participate in the event.

Our sense of fairness and equity counts much on our moral development. Whether we learn from our parents, teachers, or society, our belief in justice dictates to what extent we execute principles of fairness in our daily lives. In some situations, fairness is easier to judge and relatively clear-cut, whereas in other situations, judgements are more difficult to make. In competitions of sports, there are clear rules in place to ensure fair play. It seems easier for people to act fair, as all they basically need to do is follow the rules. Still, issues like drug use and other cheating tricks occasionally arise. Therefore, the execution of fairness is more than complying with rules. We have to do more, such as:

- Value fair chances.
- Treat people with equity and apply the same principles to everyone.
- Avoid double standards.
- Self-reflect and take perspectives of others when judgements of fairness are difficult to make. Remember that your standard of fairness might not be right all the time.

- Avoid being discouraged when people around us are unfair. We shouldn't merely lower our standards to adjust to the environment but try to help lift the standard of our groups in terms of fairness and equity.

Integrity and honesty: Integrity and honesty are about truthful presentation of oneself to others. What's on the inside is displayed on the outside. People with this strength are true to themselves and present their feelings and thinking genuinely. Their behaviours are coherent with their values. They take responsibility for their words, feelings, and behaviours. They are committed to maintaining integrity even in situations where doing the opposites was easier. Integrity is about one's courage to remain truthful when the alternatives are more tempting. Integrity makes us feel right and good about our integral selves. It is also a key ingredient of trust and thus is important in establishing trustful relationships.

In the field of sports, integrity of individual athletes is important to keep the sport clean without cheating behaviours. The doping case of Lance Armstrong, who was once a very respectable cycling champion, was a wake-up call. Not only did it have a devastating impact on the image of cycling, but it also shook the entire sports industry. People were so disappointed that they became more sceptical and started questioning the cleanness of almost every sport. Such a blow may have a positive side, though. The sporting authorities have become more precautious. Athletes more readily accept stringent rules imposed on them because they are aware of how such dishonest cases can damage their own sports.

Aside from safeguarding the cleanness of sports, there is another reason for athletes to maintain their personal integrity. Athletes, especially elite ones, are continuously under the spotlight. Media and specialists surround them all the time. Constantly being judged by others with mixed opinions, they can easily get confused and lose sight of their own characters. Some may lose track of their true selves on their way to success or failure. Remember, only authentication of self can bring forth authentic happiness. Therefore, athletes with integrity usually find their careers more manageable and enjoyable.

Drawing enormous attention from the public, Federer has adjusted himself here and there throughout his tennis career. There was a time when he got confused and struggled. As reported in an article written by the *Sunday Times* in 2004[26], Federer explained the difficulty in the initial stage of his career: 'I had been kind of faking my way through the tour. I knew how good I was, but maybe I thought I was better than I really was. I thought I had to show something, to create something new for the tour, to hit unbelievable shots at every moment for the crowd. This was kind of a mad thing in my brain, showing off instead of playing it simple sometimes. I was not concentrating enough, and I was too concerned with what people were saying and thinking about me. I was also reading the press a lot, which was killing me.' However, he did go through a mentality change by holding more on to his true self. 'I had to have fun on the court,' Federer said. 'I had to enjoy myself again, go out there and pump the fist, even though when I did it in my early days, it wasn't really me; it was a bit of a fake. But it's not fake anymore. Now I really feel it's me when I'm pumping the fist. It's natural. And I allow myself to get angry again because that's still me. I found the freedom inside myself. I found peace with myself. Just by being myself.'

Federer has taken integrity and honesty seriously, and he is not willing to forego such qualities for the sake of meeting others' demands or expectations. In 2004, Federer started to have a taste for his role change after becoming a world champion. But he wanted to keep his private part unchanged. He said, 'Off court, I definitely haven't changed. You're always going to keep your character and the way you are. People like you, or maybe they don't. But your true friends, they know who you are, and I don't think you should change towards them.'[27]

Tim Henman, a British tennis player and a good friend of Federer's, echoed later that he did not sense much change in Federer ever since Federer overtook the number one spot. Henman said, 'I think anybody who has known him for a long, long time would say it is the same person. Probably that stands out because maybe it hasn't been the same with other people in the past.'[13] Federer's unusually nice attitude towards the media once raised some doubts. Federer explained, 'If I start fighting with them [the media], or get in a mood not to answer their questions, this is when I can get into problems … I am who I am and really don't try to change for the media.'[13]

One thing that does not change much over time is Federer's natural expression of his emotions. People do appreciate Federer's tears of joy during victories. At his first triumph at Wimbledon, after sinking to his knees on the ground and doing all the hand shaking rituals, his tears flowed uncontrollably when he looked up at the audience and went back to sit on his chair. At the trophy presentation, he tried to hold back his tears but surrendered when he talked about his childhood dream and when he thanked his supporters. The following morning, he told people why: 'I'm the kind of guy who lets the tears flow, and I think that goes down pretty well, especially when people see this is the realisation of my biggest dream and that it's amazing for me. I get a lot of feedback that people in the crowd also cried and enjoyed it, and it's nice to share this with a lot of people.'

Three years later, even when he won his seventh Grand Slam at the Australian Open in 2006, his joyful tears had not yet dried. When he wiped his eyes during his emotional speech after the win, people were pleased by feeling Federer's passion for the game, including Rod Laver, who presented Federer the trophy. In 2011, thirty-year-old Federer, having won nearly seventy titles, still had moist eyes during the trophy presentation after winning his hometown title in Basel for the fifth time. He was clearly moved by the standing ovation the crowd gave their hometown hero.

However, critics came on board when Federer dropped tears of frustration uncontrollably after his loss to Nadal in the Australian Open 2009. It was a bit pathetic that some people became critical of his open emotions when he experienced tough times, saying that it signalled his weakening spirit. However, Federer himself showed no regrets in expressing his emotions, as it was natural for him. Jim Courier and Tim Henman, retired professional tennis players, simply could not understand the critics either. Jim Courier said, 'I think what we know by now about Roger is that not only is this a sensitive guy, but he is [also] incredibly emotional about the history of the game.'[28] Henman appreciated the integrity of Federer and said, 'I beat Federer in the final at Basel three or four years ago, and he was crying his eyes out. When he won Wimbledon in 2003, he was bawling his eyes out. He's just a really emotional guy. He's honest enough to say "This is who I am".'[29] In an interview done by the *Basler Zeitung* in 2009, Federer was asked if he was ever ashamed of his tears. He responded easily: 'No, not ashamed. It was perhaps a little embarrassing. The camera likes to focus closely on the tears. It is good to show emotions. I am actually happy that I do.'

A person with integrity is more trustworthy to others. Yves Allegro, who has been Federer's doubles partner and long-time friend, shared an incident that revealed Federer's accountability. Back in early 2003, Federer agreed to play an exhibition match with Allegro in mid-July at the Grone tennis club, which was owned by Allego's father. A few months later, Federer won his first Grand Slam title at Wimbledon, which was followed by tremendous media responsibilities. Despite obvious exhaustion, Federer committed to participate in a Gstaad tournament right after Wimbledon, when many people expected withdrawal. He not only showed up but also reached the final of the tournament. He was defeated, as he apparently ran out of gas. People at Grone lost hope for Federer's participation in the exhibition, which would take place only two days after the Gstaad final, considering Federer might have become either too big-headed or too exhausted for the event. Allegro, however, was convinced that Federer would show up. He strongly believed that Federer would come unless there was something unavoidable that would prevent it. Federer did deliver his promise and played a three-set exhibition match for free, helping the club to clear its debts and also giving the small-town population a memorable night.[15]

Talking about honesty, I think the greatest challenge comes when honesty stands against something we desperately want to achieve. In a tennis match, ideally, it is umpire's job to make the right calls and ensure the match is played fairly. In reality, it happens quite often that players and the umpire disagree on some calls. The Hawkeye system is now in place in many tournaments to ensure fair chances for players to challenge the calls. The battlefields left without Hawkeye are the clay courts, where the marks on the clay may dictate the ultimate calls. People who have seen Federer play on clay courts should be familiar with moments where Federer gave away points to his opponents by reporting to the umpire wrong calls that actually favoured him. A round of applause from the crowd often followed his honest moves.

Federer does not only do this in smaller tournaments or less critical moments. I remembered seeing Federer do the same on several points during some tight matches on his way to pursue his first French Open crown in 2009. During those moments, I murmured to myself, 'Oh, Roger, please don't give any free points like that at such important matches.' Since I desperately wanted him to win the missing slam at that time, I kind of got lost myself. But Federer did not lose it despite the fact that he should be the most desperate one.

I also remember a scene in another match when his opponent, David Ferrer, served his ball to the net. Federer declared to the umpire that he was not yet in a ready position when the opponent served. According to the rule, the opponent was given his first serve chance again. Ferrer immediately thanked Federer for his honesty. Federer remained as honest as he could be and stayed firm on keeping equity on court. Of course, he is not the only player demonstrating such a quality on court. I am happy to see the majority of the players backing fair play on court nowadays.

On the one hand, Federer fully understands and appreciates his status as a role model. On the other hand, he does not feel too pressured, for he believes he just needs to be his honest self. The dramatic scandal of Tiger Woods about his marital infidelity at the end of 2009 significantly lessened Tiger's status as a role model. Federer said he did not feel any particular pressure to stay clean as a result. 'I just try to be myself, not change for the press or the public or the fans,' he said. He said it was most important to him that he upheld the principles of fair play, had respect for the game and his rivals, and was polite to people he met. 'Those are key things my parents have taught me,' Federer said. Federer was also mindful of presenting his true self while avoiding growing arrogance in him. In an interview by the *Times* in June 2010[30], Federer commented on his talent and said, 'You always have to be very careful not to come across as arrogant or, like, the other way, by saying "Oh, I'm not that talented; I don't know how I've done it; I'm incredibly lucky" – so you walk a fine line. It's important to stay humble, but sometimes you have to accept who you are.' In another interview conducted in 2012 with journalist Laurent Favre from the magazine *L'Illustré*[31], Federer restated his philosophy about being authentic: 'Trying to please everyone gets you caught in a vicious circle where you only think about what others say or think about you,' he said. 'Whenever I try to do something that doesn't fit me, it makes me feel bad and under pressure. It's unpleasant.'

Cultivation of integrity and honesty comes from one's upbringing environment. Parents have the earliest chances to foster integrity in their children. Apart from teaching children to be honest with perspectives of morality, parents should reinforce children about their honest behaviours and encourage children to express their true feelings and thoughts. Of course, parents should also be good role models and take responsibility for their words and behaviours.

As grown-ups, how are we supposed to improve such qualities further? Here are some suggestions:

- We should understand more about our own emotions and beliefs.
- We should not be shy in showing our genuine emotions.

- We should not try to impress others to be someone we are not.
- We should tell the truth.
- We should keep our promises.
- We should take responsibility for our behaviours.
- We should know that inauthentic behaviours can sometimes make life easier, but only in the short run, while truthful behaviours can enhance social relationships and long-term life satisfaction.
- We should engage ourselves in social environments that reward integrity.

Humility and modesty: People who are humble and modest have correct senses of their abilities and positions. They do not seek the spotlight or stand way above their statuses. They do not feel the need to dominate others. They simply let their accomplishments speak for themselves and take credit and compliments only when they think they deserve to. They have low senses of entitlement and are not particularly fond of receiving special treatment. They know and do not mind telling others about their mistakes and limitations. Humility and modesty allow people to be able to appreciate accomplishments and contributions of others. Sportsmanship demands that athletes respect others in the field, including their competitors, whether in situations where they win effortlessly or get beaten up brutally. Often the bad winners and losers are those who fail to register humility in their personalities. Humility helps athletes refrain from growing arrogance that hurts their respectability and eventually their careers.

A common commentary about Federer is that he is very Swiss. Having been born and raised in Switzerland, Federer has been shaped by the modest nature of his culture. Swiss people are naturally modest and low-key. People from his home country are definitely proud of Federer's achievements and are more than happy to have had such an admirable Swiss tennis champion for so long. However, they seldom do hero-worshipping kinds of things. They appreciate the champion but do not say so aloud. Federer's old school and tennis clubs are not at all tempted to make a big deal out of Federer. There is no plaque or poster of Federer hanging along the school corridors. In sports stores, you do not see big posters of Federer everywhere. Making big money out of publicising someone is not something they normally do. The celebration reception of Olympic gold medallists, including Federer and Wawrinka, in 2008 was no big show, with crazy people screaming and running around. The party was unpretentious, warm, and homey.

Switzerland is a place that respects privacy and does not make a big deal for the sake of arousing public interest. Switzerland has taken much burden off Federer's shoulder as a celebrity. 'It's good we don't have paparazzi in Switzerland. We don't have people chasing you around and stuff. That's a good thing. This is one of the reasons why I want to live there when I'm older,' Federer said in an interview with *Inside Tennis Magazine* in 2008.[32] Federer's wedding in 2009 was a well-kept secret until the official announcement was made. There was no early slip of information. The wedding turned out to be a homey gathering of families and close friends, with all the blessings Federer hoped for. Federer later expressed his gratitude to the Swiss culture. 'If you want to get married in private, you have to go to Switzerland. They don't actually care over there. They actually want to give you peace and privacy. That's why I love being a Swiss and living in Switzerland.'[33]

Basel, where Federer was born, is a quiet and simple city. Federer can live quite normally in the city. He was seen walking along the street unimpeded. The neighbourhood saw him hauling his laundry basket, shopping at grocery shop, and washing his Mercedes. I think the Swiss culture should take some credit for Federer's normality despite enjoying enormous admiration around the globe.

Because he manifests humility so consistently, Federer could be called Mr Humble. He earned such a reputation earlier when he emerged to prosper, and he has been able to keep it widely affirmed throughout the periods of his rise, dominance, and slip.

Humble about his game: All people in the tennis world have been singing praises about Federer's stylish and classy tennis for many years. Federer himself acknowledges his talent and all-rounded competence in tennis, but he does not attempt to distinguish himself above all the other players. He is fully aware and appreciative of other players' strengths and efforts. Even when he faces lower ranked players in the early rounds, he senses the danger and takes the matches seriously. He gives forthright comments about his matches. In his victories, he does not gloat at all. He honestly tells what he does well in the matches, without downplaying the opponents. In his losses, he makes sure he gives enough credit to the opponents.

Federer often defends other players when they do not get the proper respect. In an on-court interview during the 2009 Australian Open, he pointed out that Andy Roddick had not been given enough credit. He himself credited Roddick for being one of his generations who had been able to stay at a top level for such a long time (Roddick had been in the top 10 ten seven years at that point). He said, 'That's rock solid. That's why I'm excited to play against him and seeing him create an upset in a big tournament.'

Federer makes generous comments about uprising players as well. In the press conference after Federer won his fifth consecutive US open in 2008, a journalist asked Federer why he always seemed to speak with tremendous sportsmanship, especially about some of the younger players coming up through the rankings. The journalist wondered if Federer, as a representative of the sport, felt it a responsibility to do so. 'No, I mean, it's up to me to be honest. I'm a very honest guy. If I think a guy is good, I'll let you know. If I think the guy is average, I'll let you know that, too,' Federer said.

Having a correct sense of his position in the tennis game, Federer never becomes too carried away by his dominance. In 2005, when his ranking lead widened against the rest of the group, he told the press, 'Maybe the difference is big in the rankings, but I feel they're all right there to beat me when I'm maybe just a little bit off. I don't see myself that far away. I know that right now I'm winning those matches, but it can turn around very quickly.' When Federer won his seventh Grand Slam title in the 2006 Australian Open, he wept uncontrollably in the speech as if it were his first. 'I don't forget that it's been a tough road for me. I amaze myself every time I do well,' he said later, explaining his emotions. Federer genuinely believes his success is not just meant to be, and he can be vulnerable at times.

Players in the locker room have high regard for Federer in this aspect. James Blake is one of those. He complimented Federer during the Miami tournament in 2009. 'I didn't feel like before he [Federer] was looking down on people, where he's better than anyone else or he's above picking up his own trash or tossing out his dirty towels or anything. He's always been just a very down-to-earth guy ... I don't think it will change no matter what the circumstances are on the court. I like the fact that I think that's just the way he was raised ... to be a polite, respectful guy. I credit him with that because a lot of people in his position could have lost that along the way.'

The cream-coloured blazer that Federer wore to Centre Court of Wimbledon raised the eyebrows of many people. Mike Bryan, a famous American doubles player, did not think that many players could be given a free pass by the guys in the locker room to wear a sport coat out to play a match. He, however, admitted that Federer carried it well because Federer was such a humble champion and friendly person that nobody thought he had a big head just because he was wearing a jacket.

Humble in front of tennis history: Before the case was more settled when he broke Sampras's slam record in 2009, there was so much debate about whether Federer has been the greatest tennis male player of all time (GOAT). I have read many different opinions from journalists, other players, and the legends of tennis. Supportive statements had the upper hand, though some opinions were more reserved. Federer feels honoured to be called the GOAT, but he never deliberately attempts to claim the honour. He is clearly not obsessed with it. His respect for tennis history and legends are genuine and widely recognised.

In 2005, after losing to Federer in the US Open final, Andre Agassi named Federer as the best player he had faced in his two-decade career, even above Pete Sampras, his long-time rival. Federer was flattered but declined to accept the compliment. He said, 'That's nice of Andre. But honestly, you can't forget about Sampras. At his best, nobody would want to play him. You can't forget about the former stars. It might be true that I'm making records and I'm dominating. It might be true that the most recent champions have a higher level because the level of tennis keeps advancing. But I'm not forgetting about the others. Just look at the records that some guys have. I'm a little cookie.'

When Federer won three slams in a roll in 2005, people started talking about the possibility of his getting the Grand Slam (winning all four Grand Slam titles in a year). Federer responded, 'If you look at history, you will see that the Grand Slam is almost impossible to achieve.' He was clearly aware of how hard the legends made the records. Australian Rod Laver, the only man who won the Grand Slam twice, has been considered one of the greatest tennis players for a long time. He said in an interview that he would be honoured to be compared to Federer. He considered Federer an unbelievable talent and said Federer could be the greatest tennis player of all time. Federer appreciated the nice comments from Laver. 'It's incredible for someone of that stature, with that incredible record, to be saying such nice things about you,' he said.

Federer enjoys meeting the legends. He gets excited and fascinated every time he meets the legends, as if he is just one of their little fans. He attributed the emotions he showed in the victory speech of the Australian Open in 2006 largely to the presence of Rod Laver. When he thanked Laver for presenting the trophy, he cried and hugged Laver hard. Federer won the Australian Open again the following year, without losing a set. The last player who did this in an Australian Open was Ken Rosewall, an Australian tennis legend. In Federer's victory speech, he paid tribute to Ken. 'Ken, I am happy to be the guy who follows up on you. Thanks very much. It's a great honour,' Federer said. Obviously, the Australian crowd appreciated very much Federer's respect for their country's past champion.

During the Australian Open in 2007, Rod Laver reaffirmed that Federer was a modest champion despite, in his opinion, that he was on his way to becoming the greatest player of all time. 'He [Federer] is so good, he could begin to think he's above everyone else, but he views himself as part of this great sport, and that's something I respect,' Laver said. Laver wrote an article that included his impression of Federer from their encounters. 'Every time I speak to Roger, I sense no ego on his part. He asks me questions about how I prepared for big matches – Roger has a clear appreciation for the history of tennis. When you're talking to Roger, he makes you feel important – whether you're a fan, an opposing player, or an old geezer like me. One thing is for sure: he's the best player of his time and one of the most admirable champions on the planet. That's certainly something worth crowing over. The beauty is, Roger Federer won't.'[34]

Pete Sampras is another tennis legend who has high praises for Federer. At the end of 2007, having twelve Grand Slams on hand, Federer was two slams short of equalling Sampras's record of fourteen. Talking about the possibility of his record being broken, Sampras gave a frank answer. 'Did I want my record to stand forever? Absolutely. Having the record was something I really strove for, and worked so hard for, but I really don't mind that it's someone like Roger breaking my record.' While Sampras appeared to be ready to let go of his record, he felt that Federer himself was not ready to be called the greatest yet. 'I don't think that Roger is at all comfortable with how great he is,' Sampras said. 'Roger and I were talking about this a few weeks ago, the debate about who is the greatest tennis player in history, and he found the whole conversation really uncomfortable. Roger isn't playing tennis for the limelight, for the pat on the back, and for the medal at the end of the race. He plays tennis because he loves tennis, and he is competitive when he gets out there on the court, but I don't think he's doing it for the praise and to be called the greatest.[35] 'He [Federer] lets his racket do the talking. He loves his tennis. He's a humble, understated man,' said Sampras during the 2008 US Open.

If you followed Federer's press conferences and interviews close enough, you would be well educated about the history of the tennis greats. His continuous breaking of records brought up those names from time to time. Federer likes to talk about tennis legends; it's as if he feels obligated to remind the public of the forgotten heroes. When he won his sixth World Tour Final titles, surpassing Ivan Lendl and Pete Sampras's record, he did not want to overshadow their achievements. 'I still don't feel like I'm better than Pete Sampras, or Lendl, for that matter,' Federer said. 'I still believe they are one of the all-time greats to play the game. I'm just happy to be compared to them. I'm actually happy that they are mentioned while I'm doing this because they have done amazing things in our sport. Sometimes legends are forgotten rather quickly, which is unfortunate. So for me to hear we are talking about Pete, Ivan, other players, I think is great for the sport and great for them.'

The press and the legends are clearly impressed with Federer's humility and modestly. What impressed me the most is that I sense no false modesty at all. Sometimes it is not too difficult for us to say humble words if we make them somewhat automatic and mechanical. Federer is one of a kind in that he can be honestly humble or humbly honest. He lets his accomplishments speak for themselves. He takes credit and compliments when he thinks he deserves them. He smiles and laughs at praise. His views on his own positions and games are not stereotyped but change with time after thoughtful assessment of his achievements and status, relative to the history and other players. Federer never attempts to make himself go beyond the game. He only tries to fit himself well into the game and do whatever he can do to contribute to the game. 'You should never forget that, if you go, somebody else will take your spot. Tennis will live on, but you won't. You're just there in the moment itself. You can never be bigger than the game,' Federer said on the *60 Minutes* programme in 2005.

In front of the greats, Federer has no problem at all in holding on to his modesty. True humility shows when Federer is giving the same impression to those fresh and young tennis players who are supposedly growing up idolising him. Jack Sock, a teenage American tennis player, got lucky enough to hit with Federer in some practice sessions in 2011. Jack was surprised that Federer showed so much interest in knowing about him. 'Most of our conversations have been tennis oriented, focusing on my training and history. He's always interested in finding out more about me,' he said. He described Federer as incredibly humble and generous.

No sense of entitlement: On his rise to be a tennis superstar, Federer made some adjustments here and there. For example, he scheduled his media requests more carefully, spent less time hanging out with other players in the locker rooms, and he did not stay in the Olympic Village during the Olympics, though he would have loved to. However, changes he makes have been somewhat reasonable, with no sense of entitlement or grandiosity involved. He treats people with respect, whether they are officials, players, journalists, locker room attendants, or ballboys. He never falls short of saying please and thanks.

At the Pacific Life Open in 2004, when the world number one player headed back to the players' locker room after his practice, he was stopped for his identification by a security guard, who did not recognise him. Being denied entrance, Federer did not get annoyed or anything; he just searched a bit helplessly for his badge in his tennis bag until a friend helped him out by telling the guard that he was the number one tennis player in the world.

Federer calmly said, 'He was only doing his job.'[36] Federer does not fall into an assumption that other people should recognise him and treat him differently.

'I don't need special treatment,' Federer explained when he was queried on an occasion about his 'weird' behaviour – at the NASDAQ-100 Open in 2005, instead of calling for a limo or golf cart, Federer walked alone and carried his heavy tennis bag across the grounds to his match and autographed for whoever asked on his way. Federer was also praised for his composed manner when he and his group were turned away from a restaurant in Lake Zurich. He calmly left without abusing his status. 'I knew I was too late,' Federer said later. I think Federer's 'normal' behaviours sometimes have been a bit overly complimented. I guess people are just too used to the grandiosity of some other superstars, making Federer's behaviours appear abnormal. Still, we have to credit Federer for apparently having no sense of entitlement.

Down-to-earth lifestyle: While Federer is so extraordinary on court, he is utterly ordinary off it. His entourage includes mainly Mirka, family and friends. He does not surround himself with publicists or bodyguards. He is comfortable with his low maintenance and down-to-earth life. His life remains very much grounded. Media sometimes complain that his quiet private life has left them so little to write about – no crazy parties, no hanging around with models and stuff like that. His hobbies are mainly shopping, text messaging, having nice meals, listening to rock music, and playing cards. During off seasons, he either stays at home in the country hanging out with family and friends or has a relaxing vacation with Mirka on a beach. Mirka still does the cooking, cleaning, and laundry herself. He and Mirka spend time washing their cars at their apartment. They go shopping for groceries like normal couples do. He loves Switzerland and Australia because he likes the down-to-earth people there.

Federer does not play tournaments to chase money. He is selective in his sponsorship deals. Even though Federer now owns several cars, of which many were championship prizes, he is clearly no materialist. A funny incident happened when he was a junior player. He was asked about how he would spend his first prize money, and the answer that was published was 'a Mercedes'. Lynette, Federer's mother, obviously knew enough about Federer that she suspected a misunderstanding was made. She listened to the recording of the interview and clarified that Federer's response was in fact '*mehr* CDs', German for 'more CDs'.[15]

'I think what he's accomplished is great, but he's not an idol, a world star, or a superhero for me,' said Patty Schnyder, one of Federer's early junior rivals.[15] 'Whenever we see each other, he's still the same guy as when we first met.' Madeleine Barlocher, who held the programme at Old Boys Tennis Club (where the young Federer received tennis training), said nice words about Federer. 'He's never looked down his nose at people. He's not made any big story, not tried to make himself popular. He's generous. And he has remained Roger.'[14] Federer tried to explain why he remained grounded despite his accomplishments at the pre-tournament conference of Indian Wells in 2007. He credited it to the good timing of his success and personal growth. 'I've gone through very interesting phases in the last ten years, tried to get to the top and staying at the top and facing many different things,' Federer said. 'Media, sponsor, fans, big occasions. And for me, I've never had a reason to kind of get crazy about it. I kind of had enough time to grow into the position because I didn't come up through juniors and then right away won Wimbledon. It took me a few years. Maybe that was the time to allow me a lot of time to grow as a person first.'

Humility and modesty are sometimes considered to limit one's strive for success and counteract one's confidence and satisfaction. I think this is mistaken. The case of Federer clearly disputes the above argument. So let us see how we can learn from him to become more humble. Here are some suggestions:

- Reflect on our achievements from time to time and build a correct sense of our abilities.
- Acknowledge our mistakes, imperfections, and limitations.
- Don't submit ourselves to a sense of entitlement – we have to believe in fair chances and should not think or act as if we are entitled to more power or special treatment.
- Listen to the stories of the other greats.
- Appreciate the efforts and contributions of others.
- Open ourselves to others' ideas and advice.
- Keep our daily lives more or less grounded.
- Beware of false modestly.

Transcending the sport

For an athlete, I think nothing creates a more long-lasting sense of meaning than being able to transcend the sport itself. Honourable athletes are those who have brought something extra to the sport. Transcendence can be done in mainly three different ways. Firstly, an athlete with ultra-athleticism or an extraordinary style of playing can bring the sport to another level. Fellow athletes will be inspired to train to learn new skills and build up their stamina. Expert fans will be pleased and appreciate the sport even more or in some new ways. Other people will be lured to like the sport and become fans. The sport advances as a result. Secondly, a sports player can have a great influence if she can be a decent role model for kids and upcoming players. It is about boosting enthusiasm and interests. It is, more importantly, about demonstrating how the sport can be played with great sportsmanship and self-respect. Then the future of the sport is secured. Thirdly, the sport is transcended when someone uses it for great causes, such as humanitarian work and helping people in need, bringing the public's attention to global issues, and so forth.

Some people believed Federer transcended tennis just as Muhammad Ali did boxing and Tiger Woods did golf. Federer's style of play is unprecedented. His fluency of movements on court is described as dancing ballet. His elegant performance attracts millions of fans and attracts more and more people to tennis, including me. The fan base of tennis has grown enormously during the period he's played. He has certainly added a little bit of different favour to tennis.

Being inspired by his idols, Boris Becker and Stefan Edberg, during his young age, Federer recognises his responsibility of being a proper role model to inspire kids and teenagers. 'It's important to get the image right for the young. I hope to inspire kids, and it is a way of giving something back,' he said when he turned into world number one in 2004.[37]

Nice words about Federer came from some junior players who were lucky enough to get a chance to practice with the best ever player. In August 2007, Matt Allare, a teenage American player who was named high school player of the year by the National High School Coaches Association, was called in one morning by his tennis club to check for his availability to practice with Roger Federer on that day. The teenager, of course, found the invitation irresistible and hurried immediately to the club to hit balls with the top player in the world. He later revealed that it was the most amazing experience, one that he would never forget. While he was amazed by Federer's shots and tactics, he was also impressed by Federer's classy, likable manner. 'He is just a fantastic person, a really nice guy. He is a great person from what I have seen,' said Allare. When Federer ran into Allare in the lunchroom the day after they practiced together, he stopped to greet Allare by his name.[38]

Another lucky young player, seventeen-year-old Berankis, was invited by Federer to join him in Dubai for days of training before the US Open in 2007. Following the practice, Berankis won the Canadian Open Junior Championships and won the US Open Junior without losing a set. He told the press, 'I learnt many things practicing with Roger Federer, and he gave my coach many pieces of advice.'

During the tour of the Capitala World Tennis Championship, which was first held in Abu Dhabi in 2009, Federer spent some time hitting balls with a group of kids. People wondered why he enjoyed playing with those kids so much. He said, 'I love inspiring kids, trying to be a good role model. I needed an idol or a hero when I was growing up. If I can portray that, that's great. But I guess the best part of it is to play with the kids to see their excitement, help them a little bit, and motivate them to be [champions].'

Beyond his own tennis success, Federer dedicated himself to make tennis a better sport. 'I am trying to help the game, make it grow, and leave it better off than when I came,' he told *Gulf News* in an interview in 2010. Federer does not just make a wish and hope the thing will happen. He, in fact, has done more than his fair amount of work. He, as the president of ATP Player Council, together with other elected representatives, takes his time collecting opinions from players, voicing players' concerns in the meetings, and implementing improvements on the tour. Federer explained his commitment to the council. 'I would feel disappointed if I just left the game and never took an active part in trying to change it for the better. There are so many issues to talk about, and instead of being on the sideline and being critical, it is nice to be part of the process. I'd like to have an active role in the future of this wonderful game.'

Federer has been the ambassador for tennis. But he does not only care about tennis. He also cares about vulnerable populations in the world. He utilises his fame in helping people in need. ATP gave him the Federer Arthur Ashe Humanitarian Award twice to honour him for his humanitarian work through his foundation. Federer started his own Roger Federer Foundation in 2003, at the young age of twenty-two, right after he won his first Grand Slam at Wimbledon. He said, 'I've already won so much in my short tennis career. I would like to give something back with my foundation, especially to those that have the least.' As revealed by the slogan of the foundation, 'I am tomorrow's future', the mission of the foundation is to support needy children and enhance them in pursuing better futures.

The foundation has formed a collaborative relationship with a relief organisation in South Africa to help the underprivileged children in New Brighton Township, which is one of the most disadvantaged areas in South Africa. Federer has a special link with South Africa because his mother grew up there and because he visited the place with his parents many times during his childhood. He liked South Africa and found the experience enlightening. He felt that the country was a place that had overcome hatred and oppression. He wanted to help by providing practical and tangible support in a highly deprived area. While

Federer was inspired by Agassi to set up a foundation of his own in his young age, Nadal also looked upon Federer when he set up his foundation.

Beyond monetary donations and publicity showing, Federer is willing to get personally involved in helping people in need. He organised a visit to the New Brighton Township in 2005 with Mirka, his mother, and Nicola Arzani of ATP. He refused the suggestion of creating major publicity about the visit. He did not want to make a big deal out of it. He explained that the purpose of the visit was to see things for himself and to feel what it was like to live in the place. He wanted to find out how much difference his foundation had made to the lives of the people living there. He visited an AIDS hospital. He also went to schools to play soccer and basketball with the students. When he saw kids playing happily, he got emotional at seeing happiness and sadness existing so close together. Federer paid a trip to Ethiopia in 2010 to see the charitable works of his foundation there. He visited the school and was welcomed by a group of singing children. The singing moved Federer to tears. He played some table tennis and even ran a thousand-metre race. Reflecting on his trip, he said, 'It's just a nice thing to do if you can help others. Obviously, I'm in this fortunate position that I can help in a big way. And I'm very happy to do so. *I think every human who has an opportunity should give maybe something back – if it's time, if it's money, or if it's just inspiring others.*'

Federer took the lead in gathering players, as a tennis family (as Federer likes to call it), for great clauses. In 2004, Federer was deeply shocked by the tragedy caused by the tsunami that was set off by an earthquake in Indonesia. Apart from immediate donation, he wanted to contribute more. He took an empathetic initiative to organise an exhibition match with the top players in order to raise some money for UNICEF and other relief efforts. He invested his effort and time to make sure the event could be done. This was a rather special campaign in the tennis field. A bunch of top players played exhibition matches in Indian Wells, raising funds through tickets sale and even collecting donations from the stands. It was a unique event. Given that tennis is a rather individualistic sport, Federer was particularly happy that players could unite on some occasions. Although Federer's busy tennis schedule prevented him from getting too involved in regular charity work, he used his initiative to help when he felt the need.

In January 2009, the devastating earthquake in Haiti caused tens of thousands of people to die. Federer again was struck by the tragedy. Two days before the start of the first Grand Slam of the year, the Australian Open, Federer initiated an idea of organising an exhibition match for fundraising at the eve of the tournament. Given the short period of time and the possible interruptions in players' preparation for the Open, even the tennis organisation, which Federer approached for help, found it almost impossible to get it done. Yet Federer successfully made use of his good connections. He called some players himself and received encouraging responses. 'I think it's something as a tennis family we're very happy to do. I know it's on the eve of the first Grand Slam of the season, so it's for some not so easy maybe mentally to separate a few things – but I think it's a great initiative,' he said.

The exhibition event, called Hit for Haiti, was arranged in less than twenty-four hours and successfully took place at Rod Laver court of Melbourne Park, with a full crowd in attendance. Top male and female players, including Rafael Nadal, Novak Djokovic, Andy Roddick, Lleyton Hewitt, Serena Williams, Kim Clijsters, and Samantha Stosur, joined Federer's efforts. The players played doubles and mixed doubles in combinations that were rarely seen. They entertained the crowd by playing shots and making jokes. 'It was a fun afternoon for all of us. But most important is that we can help Haiti,' Federer told the centre court crowd after the match. The event raised more than AUD\$600,000, including ticket sales, after-effect donations by tennis organisations, and fundraising by selling players' rackets.

Encouraged by the event in Australia, another exhibition night, featuring double matches of Roger Federer/Pete Sampras against Rafael Nadal/Andre Agassi, and Martina Navratilova/Justine Henin against Lindsay Davenport/Steffi Graf, was organised in Indian Wells for the same cause. The second Hit for Haiti charity tennis exhibition raised US\$1 million for earthquake relief efforts. A year later, right before the Australian Open in 2011, Federer again put together a similar fundraising event called Rally for Relief, which was a charity match aimed at benefitting victims of flooding in eastern Australia. At the end of 2010, Federer and Nadal, the field's top two players, used their precious time during the off season to organise and play two charity matches together in Zurich and Madrid to raise funds for their respective foundations.

Federer was appointed as a UNICEF Goodwill Ambassador in 2006. It made perfect sense given his publicity and humanity. Acknowledging the honour and responsibility, Federer said, 'I share UNICEF's belief about sports teaching important life lessons about respect, leadership, cooperation. I believe that sports can help overcome injustice and build bridges between cultures and nations. As tennis players, we have a unique opportunity. We are given a chance to visit so many different countries and cultures and interact with people from all walks of life. It is our responsibility to connect with the real world beyond our sport, [to] use our fortune to make a difference in the lives of those who most need it. If I can make a contribution to this, I am more than happy to do so, and I am really, really looking forward to the future.' His first trip as an ambassador was to a life skills workshop in India that provided education on HIV/AIDS to the young. He said, 'I think if people can help the process, trying to make HIV a thing of the past, I'm willing to help too.'

Not only were the people in the tennis field impressed by Federer's character; admiration came from other top athletes as well. Olympic downhill skiing champion Lindsey Vonn revealed how Roger Federer inspires her, both as an athlete and as a person. As an athlete: 'The way he keeps fighting back to dominate his sport personally inspires me,' Vonn said. As a person: 'Of all the athletes I've ever met, Roger is the kindest and most genuine. He really cares about people, and what he's done with his foundation and his humanitarian efforts has been incredible. He's hard-working and extremely humble, but the thing I respect most about him is he's the same person every day whether he wins or loses. He cares about being a role model and that kids can look up to him. I consider him a hero because I want to be like him. I want to be a good role model for kids too.'

When we look at the character strengths listed earlier in this chapter, we should try to find out which ones are our signature strengths. Please do not take this wrong – that we should spend time and effort to build up *all* our strengths as much as we can. There would be too much stress and frustration involved. We are not trying to be perfect. Some people cannot enjoy life because they focus too much on their weaknesses and try too hard to remedy them. As a result, they forget about their strengths and miss the opportunities to use them.

From the perspective of positive psychology, we just need to focus more on our key strengths and explore ways to exercise them. We first identify our top three to five signature strengths, through self-reflection or feedback from somebody close to us. There is also a well-established questionnaire for identifying the signature strengths – VIA Survey of Character Strengths – developed by Dr. Seligman's team, and it is available at http://www.authentichappiness.sas.upenn.edu/. After identifying our signature strengths, we try to exercise those strengths as much as we can in the main realms of our lives, like in our families, at work, and in our social relationships. And for the sake of having a meaningful life, we may further utilise those strengths in serving something beyond our individual selves and for higher purposes.

CHAPTER 6
Accomplishment (A)

Accomplishment, as a fifth element of well-being, concerns things like success, achievement, goal attainment, competence, and mastery. It is considered one distinct component of well-being because it is believed to be pursued for its own sake, not just for the positive feelings that it can bring. Attaining goals and achieving success are probably our most innate desires. Day after day, we have so many implicit and explicit goals we want to achieve, both short term and long term. Accomplishment is about achieving longer term persistent goals. However, a sense of accomplishment does not occur only when the ultimate goal is attained; it can be felt and accumulated bit by bit intermediately. Having a sense of mastery and competence is our intrinsic need to safeguard our esteem and prove our existential value. Accomplishment directly contributes to our well-being. At the same time, it contributes indirectly by eliciting our positive emotions, such as gratification for achieving success or gratefulness for having achieved what we want.

For an athlete, achievement is somewhat measurable, as it can be assessed objectively by counting numbers of wins, trophies, records, awards, and so forth. There are world ranking systems in many kinds of sports – for example, for snooker and most racquetball games. Sports players can know exactly where they stand in the field in terms of their results. Because of the advance of technology, numerous data is available for analysis. Dozens of statistics can be generated to facilitate easier comparison intra- and inter-generationally. Quantitative measures of success enable athletes to set specific goals for themselves, should it be attaining top rankings, rewriting some records, or winning a certain number of titles.

Does it mean that an athlete winning more titles ought to feel more accomplished than one with fewer titles? Or should an athlete yielding more solid career results enjoy better well-being? Not necessarily. It's not that simple. Correlations exist, but they are probably not linear. Relative to expectation, a sense of achievement is derived from the results. If the expectation is too high to start with, results lower than it may not yield much sense of achievement. Athletes sometimes find obsession with numbers in the sports industry annoying. They refuse to judge their own careers only by figures. There are things other than the results of competitions giving them a sense of accomplishment. For example, they acquire a sense of mastery and competence during practices and trainings. They may do so even during loses if they are able to register their own capabilities and improvements. These contribute to fostering a sense of accomplishment too.

In this chapter, we are going to go through several qualities that are considered accomplishment enhancing. If we can nurture those qualities in us, we set ourselves in the right position for achieving more in our lives.

Motivation and commitment

Accomplishment, in the well-being theory, is about realising our dreams rather than achieving what others think we should do. Motivation, as the inner driver for turning our desires, wishes, or goals into plans and actions, is therefore crucial in our pursuit of accomplishment. When we are highly motivated, we feel energised to set goals and then execute our plans accordingly. Loss of motivation leads to sluggishness, procrastination, or even quitting. Intrinsic motivation, derived from fundamental motivation to learn and acquire new skills, is relatively more enduring than extrinsic motivation that comes from external rewards like grades or money.

Managing our motivation is therefore a key aspect in achieving success. A motivational boost is needed whenever our inner drive is running out of fuel. Motivation management is not easy, for it requires a great deal of self-reflection. More importantly, it is possible if and only if we are committed to our goals. Commitment means we are promising ourselves that we will be fully dedicated to what we are striving for. Commitment to life goals enables us to stay motivated and engaged in life as well as open ourselves to rewarding experiences. Achieving life goals nourishes an inner experience of stable happiness and a sense of accomplishment.

The career life of an athlete is normally so short and condensed that motivation and commitment can be quite influential. Those who succeed are usually those who are most committed to the sport and those who manage their motivation well. An occasional slip in motivation may have a rather detrimental impact on one's career accomplishment. Some lose motivation because they lose too much. Fire is burnt out or overtaken by frustration. Paradoxically, some lose motivation when they have won too much, as they are unable to keep the fire going by reinvesting themselves in new goals. As a result, they miss chances to capitalise fully on their potentials to achieve more.

Achieving success in tennis has always been one of Federer's important life goals since he started to train seriously in tennis during childhood. He knew he was talented in the sport and had already set high goals, like winning Wimbledon and attaining number one ranking, when he was in his teens. Not many people truly have the opportunity to go after their childhood dreams. Federer did, and he was clearly grateful for that. But we also have to credit Federer for his unbelievably strong commitment to the game. From time to time, some people thought that loss of motivation might be a risk factor for Federer, given his dominance and his achievements. Yet he has constantly impressed others by staying highly motivated for so long. Let us review below how Federer reflected on his motivation and commitment for the game in his tennis career.

> 2005: 'I am really in the mood to try to achieve more. I enjoy winning. I enjoy playing in front of the crowd. I like that challenge. I like to take on the other guys. I don't like to hide. I could sit at home and be number one in the world and look at the other guys and say, "You battle it out, and I'll come when it really matters …" I want to play … some smaller events. I don't like just to look at the slams as the only thing that matters. For me, it means the other tournaments, when I'm competing against the best players or playing in front of thousands of people.'[39]

2006: 'So for me, my dream came true by becoming number one in the world, winning on the big stages and so on, and I think once you've sniffed a little bit of that air out there on the big stages, you always want more of it … You can't get enough. That's what happened for me; I enjoy it so much, and I think for me to now just say "OK, now it's getting a little boring" … would be a totally wrong approach, and I don't feel this way. I'm not even happy about it because I think it's just normal that you don't get bored … I don't think it's going to change how I look at the game. I love the game no matter how it's going to turn out to be. If I'm never going to win a match again, I'll walk away and love the sport, and I think that's what matters most in the end.'[40]

2007: 'I enjoy the battle so much on the tennis court with my opponent; practice is also fun, playing in front of all the fans, enjoying the applause and everything; that's what will keep me going in tennis for at least the next five years.'[41]

2008: (This is the year that Federer suffered from mononucleosis, which impaired his performance.) 'I don't think that I'll just quit one day and retire early because I'm tired. I really don't … I understand that the hunger can begin to disappear at some point. You invest so much and, at some point, the body becomes tired. You have to go through a lot in a career. But as a boy I always dreamt of becoming number one, and it would be wrong if my drive were to fail me at this point.[42]

2009: (This is the year that Federer became a husband and a father.) 'I think it's [becoming a father] just going to be more fun even. I think it's going to motivate me and inspire me, seeing how the child grows and so forth. And Mirka's dream, especially mine too in a way, was always to maybe one day have maybe a kid on the sideline seeing me play while I'm still active. I think there's a great possibility now, and so I'm excited about that. That's why even more so I want to play for a long time.'

'I always said it doesn't matter when I retire; I'll be at peace. I can walk away from this game tomorrow, but I don't choose to, because I love this game too much.'[43]

2012: During the London Olympics in 2012, he was asked if he had any extended period where he just didn't feel like playing tennis anymore. He told the press, 'For me, no, I haven't actually had a period of time where I thought … this should be it, just because I was winning, losing, travelling. It never really came to my mind, even though I was asked a lot of questions about it.'

In terms of his tour results, 2013 was a bad year for Federer. He played the tour with lingering back injury most of the time. By the end of the year, his ranking dropped to number eight, the lowest ever for him since 2002. This probably was the year when he was asked most about a possible retirement plan. Of course, as a fan, I believed Federer should be the only one who had the right to say when he was going to put down his racket. At the end of 2013, he did put down his old racket, not to quit but for an even stronger commitment. Federer decided to play with a new racket with an enlarged frame, going from ninety square inches to ninety-eight square inches. That is the biggest possible change a tennis player can make. At age thirty-two, with his hall of fame status well in check, he was still willing to make such a big adjustment in his game in order to lengthen his tennis career. Such commitment is impressive, isn't it? Using his new racket, not only did Federer find his new drive, but he also found his A game back to achieve resurgence in his tour results. He broke right back into the top four in the first quarter of the season in 2014.

Federer believes his life is not limited to playing tennis and that he has a lot more to achieve. A happy and healthy life usually builds on attaining well-balanced life goals. Being a husband and a father, Federer appreciates his role as a family man and welcomes the challenge of taking the responsibility. Though Federer has not had his paths sorted out for his life after retiring from the professional tour, he intends to carry on and be involved more in charitable business and as an ambassador for tennis. Should Federer be as committed to these other life goals as he was to his tennis career, he has a great chance to accomplish more in other aspects of his life.

I hope you know by now how important motivation is for achieving our goals. We need to care about this before we can get anywhere close to success. Here are some tips in setting goals and dealing with motivational setbacks:

1) SMART goal setting and implementation:

- Set goals in life areas that we value much. Those goals need to be SMART (specific, measurable, achievable, realistic, and time based).
- Think thoroughly about pathways to achieve the goals and come out with concrete implementation plans.
- Evaluate the progress and adjust our plans accordingly.
- Identify the major roadblocks and develop strategies to overcome them.
- Fuel willpower with positive self-talks: 'Yes, I can do this' and 'This is what I long for.'

2) Handling motivational setbacks

- Understand that motivational setbacks are normal and inevitable.
- Just keep things going at first. No impulsive stopping or quitting.
- Determine whether we have any unrealistic fears. It can be fear of loss. It can be fear of success too. Challenge those fears and make sure we have realistic expectations.
- Plant images of succeeding in our minds.
- Review our previous achievements.
- Back up our plans by acquiring necessary skills and knowledge.

Perseverance

Perseverance is an important character strength that is closely related to accomplishment. Dealing with obstacles, some may back off or even quit, whereas some may try to overcome them with perseverance, which represents an ability to exert one's diligence to complete a task or in achieving a goal. On the pathways to our goals, there might be obstacles, difficulties, boredom, frustration, or temptation. Perseverance enables us to continue with our tasks until we meet our end goals. Even the process of persisting evokes a great sense of mastery. In sports, perseverance has additional significance, as it is regarded as one of the core values of sportsmanship. An athlete giving up in a competition is the last thing we want to see and is almost disrespectful to competitors and spectators.

Perseverance and diligence are relatively less identified qualities of Federer's. Looking so smooth and at ease on court, Federer gives an impression of a gifted player who achieves greatness solely by capitalising his talent. His hard work behind it is often overlooked. Tennis is a sport that demands players to keep performing at consistently high levels throughout a year to stay in the top spots. Without tough training, it is almost impossible to sustain top rankings. Look at the case of Marat Safin, a Russian tennis player. He was once considered a player who had so many gifts in his shots and footwork. However, he was not a guy who could follow a strict routine and maintain hard training over a long period of time. He went up and down in rankings and then was left out in top competition after winning two Grand Slams. So it is evident that Federer's stunning records could hardly be achieved without his industry and persistence.

People learnt to appreciate Federer's perseverance more when he needed to fight harder in tough matches, like winning five sets after being down one or two. Some people did notice Federer's such strength earlier. Adolf Kacovski was the one who coached the teenage Federer at the Old Boys Tennis Club. He remembered how Federer worked hard in his coaching session. 'We'd have a long coaching session, he'd work very hard, and then, when it was all over, he'd go to hit against the wall or seek out a sparring partner to hit some more.'[15]

Back in the early years, knowing what physical strength meant to his tennis, Federer started to work seriously on his fitness with his fitness trainer, Pierre Paganini. For over ten years, Federer did all sorts of fitness exercises with Paganini throughout the seasons to strengthen all the movements he played on court, especially his footwork. Paganini was surprised by Federer's motivation in the training. Paganini said, 'He never complains about having to work hard as long as he understands why he is doing it. He asks me what we are doing and why and then he gets to work. He knows that he is talented and that the fitness work we do is going to bring that talent through … Even when I am really tough on him, he never stops working and he never wants to stop. That's the kind of man he is and that's why he is a champion.'[44] Paganini was impressed that Federer worked even harder after he had already become a champion in majors. While some players found it hard to motivate themselves after they claimed big titles, Federer kept on working harder to get better, like a challenger.

Federer has been quite cautious about his physical health and does not mind taking a prolonged break when necessary. However, once he starts to play for a match, he never retires. To the best of my knowledge, during his entire professional career of over a thousand matches, Federer has never retired from a match once he stepped onto a court. This statistic about Federer is extraordinary and set a par way above his peers. Federer has sent a clear message over the years that he will not easily pull out; otherwise, he would not have walked on court. At the Orange Bowl in Florida in 1998, Federer needed to win the event to have a chance to achieve year-end number one world junior. Unfortunately, he injured his foot during a training session. Federer became serious. With his clear goal in mind, he refused to quit. He concentrated and continued to play with an injured foot. He won all the matches he needed. He lifted the trophy, the Orange Bowl, and clinched his number one world junior ranking at the end of the year.

The year-end Masters tournament features the best eight male players in the respective season and is the ultimate highlight before calling off the season. However, the tournament has been bothered much by players' withdrawals or retirements because of the fatigue and injuries the players might have accumulated through the long and tiring season. Towards the season's end in 2005, Federer tore a tendon in his right foot during a practice session. Doubt was raised about his possibility to compete in the year-end Masters Cup in Shanghai. It was very unfortunate for the event since many of the qualified players, including Andy Roddick, Lleyton Hewitt, and Marat Safin were all absent. Therefore, officials and fans greatly appreciated Federer's appearance at the event after rehabilitation; he somewhat saved the event.

In his first-round ribbon match, Federer played patchily to win against Nalbandian. After the match, a reporter asked Federer nervously if he would quit due to the injury. With a smile, Federer responded spontaneously, 'I won't quit. I can assure you.' Federer delivered his promise. He didn't quit. Andre Agassi and Rafael Nadal pulled out due to injuries the next day, and it was almost a disaster for the tournament. But Federer went on to get through to the final, despite needing to call for a physiotherapist during his match against Ivan Ljubicic. The five-set final was very much the final that officials and fans hoped for, but it was definitely torture for Federer's body. Federer was beaten in the end in terms of the match but not his fighting spirit.

Federer also had a back injury in the Shanghai Masters Cup in 2008. His third-round ribbon match against Andy Murray was extremely tense. Federer failed to go into the semi-final after his three-set loss of 6–4, 6–7, 5–7 against Murray. During the match, he called for a medical break to treat his back. The audience could practically feel the pain and tightness in his back, which made his fight against the match points in the long last game particularly impressive. In the post-match conference, one journalist raised a sensible question: 'Was there any stage in the match when you considered quitting?' Federer's answer was clear and firm, 'I don't quit once I step on court. Guess you have to drill me one in the eye, then maybe. But otherwise I don't quit.'

Several tough losses marked Federer's season in 2011. The toughest of all was his semi-final loss to Djokovic in the US Open, where he lost in five sets from a two sets up lead and could not seize his chances on two match points. The match took away his last chance of saving his season by winning a major after failed attempts in three previous majors and ended his streak of winning at least one major each year since 2003. After the match, I left a message on Federer's home page to show my support as a fan and help bring Federer's perseverance to fans' attention:

> We should all appreciate Roger for battling so hard against
> players of a new generation, against aging, against slowing
> surface, against harsh comments, and against unbelievably
> high expectations. He could have retired and enjoyed his

status and life comfortably. But he welcomes the challenge. He loves the game very much. He plays for the game and his fans. He has never retired from a match, except for a single walkover, in his entire career. He bears pain and fatigue to do so. Huge respect is warranted.

Perseverance and diligence give us a better chance of achieving challenging goals and deriving greater satisfaction from subsequent success. With the experience of putting in hard work and overcoming obstacles, we sharpen our skills and increase our self-confidence. To build up such strengths, we may try the following:

- Engage ourselves in tasks or activities that require sustained effort and persistence, such as a long-term project, a study course, or a marathon.
- Set goals and plans in some important areas of our lives and stick to them.
- Do not give up easily. Dismiss our quitting thoughts consciously.
- Do not count on extrinsic rewards to keep our motivation. Focus more on substantiating our intrinsic rewards – for example, sense of pleasure, satisfaction, and esteem.
- Perceive failures as learning opportunities on our route to attaining goals.
- Give meaning to our effort and believe that the effort will finally pay off.
- Value and enjoy the process as much as the results.
- Sharpen our time management and problem-solving skills.

Self-control

People often consider self-control more of a need than a strength. It is easily left out when people think about their own strengths and weaknesses. Self-control is about the ability to exert control over certain responses, including thoughts, emotions, impulses, performances, and other behaviours. Such control is performed in the purpose of achieving higher goals and for the good sake of self or others. People who are good at self-regulation have higher self-esteem and enjoy better interpersonal relationships.

To get an idea of how self-control can help one's career in sports, we can refer to an interesting evolution of Federer from a young boy with frequent tantrums to a man who shows decent composure on and off the tennis court. Federer was well known for his loss-of-control tantrums on court during his junior years, which was signified by his throwing and breaking his rackets during frustrating moments in a match. Being aware of how his negative emotions on court might hurt his tennis, the junior Federer sought help from a sports psychologist. He recalled the experience later in an interview. 'I was getting too upset, so I needed some help on how to think about different things and how to get rid of the feelings of anger. That's why I worked with the psychologist. I think I've always been told the right things from the people around me: things like how to behave, how hard to work, what to do, what not to do. But in the end, it's [you] who has to react and want to put in the effort,' he explained. 'After working with the psychologist, I kind of worked on it myself.' With conscious effort, he later evolved to become a man who could keep his emotions inside during competition in order to maintain his focus in a match. Such growth in self-control helps him to maintain extraordinary consistency in his game during his tennis career.

On the tennis court, many factors can put a player at risk of wavering or losing concentration. Disturbing factors are things like sunlight, heavy winds, shouting from crowds, injuries, and perhaps most significantly, one's own destructive thoughts. Federer has been renowned for keeping calm and collected in a match. He looks up at his player box much less than all other players on the tour. He believes that it is his responsibility to control his game, emotions, and thoughts throughout the matches.

Many people who understand tennis find Federer's record of twenty-three consecutive semi-finals at Grand Slams scary and non-human. Of course, they are bewildered by how Federer has consistently played at such a high level. Another mystery is how Federer can be free of serious injury in all the slams across so many seasons in a row. Self-control explains part of it. Federer does what it takes to preserve his body for prolonging his tennis career against a stream of younger and more powerful challengers. Again, he will take a prolonged break if he feels he needs to. He knows what his body tells him, and he plans and controls his schedule accordingly. Federer's physical trainer, Mr Paganini, is surprised by Federer's perfect combination of creativity and discipline. It is not rare to see talented players become underachievers due to their loss of control and erratic acts.

Without a full-time coach at some stages of his tennis career, Federer has only a small entourage, including Mirka and parents, with himself always being in the lead. He makes his own decisions about his tour, media requests, and sponsorship obligations. He has high autonomy as well as self-discipline. 'In our job, the physical and the mental strengths have to be there, and the private life has to be intact so you don't lose your mind during changeovers and start thinking about weird stuff,' Federer said. He gave up some of his other interests to safeguard for his health; for example, he decided to stay away from skiing and golf. He believes that these can come later in his life. He turned down many sponsorship offers because he realised the time and commitment they would take and what that would mean to his tennis career. 'You have to have the work ethic, the professional side of things, to sleep, drink, live healthy as a tennis player, because no one else is running but ourselves. We have no substitute,' Federer said at the ATP World Tour Finals in 2011.

Discipline is based very much on sense of responsibility. In 2004, Federer came to the Australian Open without a coach. He started to take full responsibility of his own practice and tour schedule. After fulfilling interview requests the week before the Australian Open, he decided to take Sunday, the eve of the Open, off from media duties. Many of the Swiss press showed up on Sunday and found out that they missed the chance to interview Federer. They were obviously unhappy. Federer then did something that a player normally would leave to someone else, whether agent or coach. He told the International Tennis Federation's officer that he would deal with the issue himself. He explained to the Swiss press about his need to take a day off and asked for their respect. His sense of responsibility was well displayed in his leave-it-to-me attitude.

In 2007, due to fatigue he felt after the French Open, Federer decided to withdraw from the tournament in Halle. Instead of getting his agent to pass on the message, which was what other players usually did, Federer called the Halle tournament director himself to explain the situation. His responsible attitude earned the director's understanding. The tournament also earned the reward of having Federer sign a deal to play the tournament for three years, from 2008 to 2010.

On a special night during the French Open tour in 2010, Federer honoured a promise to attend an International Tennis Federation awards dinner. The night should have been a different taste for Federer, as only a few hours before the dinner, he lost his quarter-final match in the French Open Slam, which ended his road to defend the title and also his semi-final streak at slams. Federer would have been forgiven for giving the dinner a miss. However, he showed his class by showing up at the dinner, giving the necessary speech, and posing for pictures. His appearance at the dinner caught the guests by surprise, and they greeted Federer with standing ovations and deep appreciation.

Maybe the term 'self-control' gives people an impression of involving too much restraining of oneself. Let me clarify. What we are discussing here is about how people can self-regulate themselves better to meet and balance their various needs and goals as well as prevent life from getting out of control. Now see what we can do to keep all different aspects of our lives intact and on track:

- Increase self-awareness: Conflicting or obscure standards undermine self-regulation, and therefore we need to review our needs and goals from time to time and get an idea of where we stand against those.
- Learn to control our impulses: We do not live every moment according to plan. We experience different kinds of impulses from time to time. Impulses are normal products of human minds. They can be bad ideas yet can be pretty cool and creative sometimes. How we respond to our impulses makes the big difference. Immediate

gratification of our impulses usually does more harm than good. We have to learn to hold back our impulses and study the consequences of acting on them. Then we decide whether we should stick to our original plans or adjust our plans accordingly.

- Grow our sense of responsibility: Don't be afraid of taking a little bit more responsibility, whether at work, with family, and so on. Responsibility helps train our self-control. When we make ourselves accountable to someone or something with bigger purposes, we will give more thought to our responses and carry ourselves better, having a controlled manner.

Resilience

In my opinion, the quality that is needed most for us to accomplish something in our lives is resilience – how well we handle adversities and rebound from our life lows. Adversities are inevitable in our lives. Exam failure, loss of a job, breakup of a relationship, illness, and death of a loved one are only some examples. How we deal with our adversities considerably affects our life growth. Stressful life experiences can be damaging if one fails to cope with them, but they can also provide opportunities for personal growth if one is able to cope well and ride it out. Resilience is not something extraordinary. It is supposed to be a quality that everyone can normally demonstrate, at least to a certain degree. Of course, some people are more readily able to rebound from difficult times, while some could get themselves stuck in holes for longer or forever. What makes the differences? Fortunately, resilience is not considered completely an inborn trait. It is believed to be a set of attitudes and skills that can be learnt and developed.

Hardiness is a key ingredient of resilience. It is about one's positive capacity to cope with stress and catastrophe. It comprises mainly three important living attitudes: *commitment, control, and challenge (the 3Cs)*. Commitment refers to having a clear purpose and active engagement in life. When you commit, you believe in staying involved with the people and events around you rather than pulling out. It makes you hang on through your tough moments, not giving up easily.

The control component is about one's belief in self-ability to manage and influence the courses and outcomes of life events. High self-efficacy empowers people to turn things around amid adversities.

The challenge component addresses how we perceive the changes in life. When we perceive a change as a threat, as driven by a natural instinct, we tend to be frightened and run away from it. Alternatively, we can perceive change or even a downturn as a challenge and believe that challenge is part of a normal life and an opportunity for growth. When we view our adversities as challenges, positive self-growth can be achieved by overcoming them.

Apart from hardiness, hope and optimism are also significant contributing factors in resilience. Hopelessness and pessimism destroy one's motivation to move on and dampen one's faith in turning things around. When we are hopeful, we can keep our goals in sight and find the right pathway to reach our goals. When we are optimistic, we believe bad things just happen, without blaming ourselves too much or generalising the demon, thus preserving our faiths in rebounds from our downturns.

Two quotes from Federer best exhibited the proper mindset for being resilient. In 2007, the tennis world was clouded by players betting on tennis games, which called for match-fixing controversy. Because he cared extremely about the cleanness of the sport, Federer was clearly bothered by the issue. Despite the hassle, he expected the sport to bounce back from the difficult year quickly, supported by his belief: 'I always believe if you're stuck in a hole and maybe things aren't going well, you will come out stronger. Everything in life is this way'.[45]

In February 2009, shortly after Federer left Melbourne with a painful five-set loss at the slam final, he talked to the press, Xpress, and explained how he got over the loss. 'You can't win everything. The idea is to take positives from those setbacks and work at getting better.'[46] To sum it up, in Federer's rule book, to rebound from life lows, people need to take positives from setbacks and believe that they will come out stronger.

Federer has his way of digesting his defeats to stay positive and move on. When he lost his quarter-final match at Roland Garros in 2010, which was the first time in six years that he was defeated before the semi-final in slams, he also faced the threat of losing his number one ranking as a result of the defeat. It was somewhat crucial, as he would have at least tied Sampras's record of weeks at number one should he came through to the semi-final. I remember being so worried about Federer's ranking that I almost hoped Nadal would lose right away in his next match to keep Federer's number one ranking alive. Then I read Federer's comments after the match, and I admired his attitude. Federer refused to take on too much from the match loss. He said, 'You just take the defeat as it is. You don't think of the consequences.' Patrick McEnroe, an ESPN analyst, appreciated Federer's handling of his defeats. 'He's really good about shaking off losses,' McEnroe said.[47] 'He doesn't let those things stay with him that long. He's a great adapter and a great adjuster.'

Now let us walk through some of Federer's defining moments that best showed his resilience. We can pay special attention to see how he counted on his 3Cs and positive mindset to come back up every time he hit his lows.

Glorious rebound to attain the status of 'GOAT'

How Federer dominated the men's tennis world in his decade was no doubt amazing. But what I found exceptionally enchanting was his rebound from what was seemingly a down year for him in 2008 to a status where he became more securely regarded as the greatest player of all time ('GOAT') in 2009. During these two special years, Federer's fans felt as if they were riding on a roller coaster. The tennis world was so unsure of what to expect from Federer that the commentaries moved sideways and were very inconsistent. In 2008, Federer was beaten in the first three slams, which included the ending of his reign at Wimbledon. He won fewer titles than he used to and failed to win a Masters Series tournament in the whole season. He lost his number one position, which he'd held for a record 237 consecutive weeks. The only positive highlights of his year were the US Open title and the Beijing double gold medal in the last quarter of the season.

During the year, the sayings about Federer's career decline had, to some extent, crowded out the encouraging words from his supporters. There were people so eager to write him off as if they did not want to be the last ones to make the right call. Yet the call was proved to be totally wrong. In 2009, Federer did almost all the things he was supposed to do to ensure his GOAT place in tennis history. He completed his career Grand Slam by winning the French Open. He broke Sampras's Grand Slam record by winning his fifteenth Grand Slam title at Wimbledon. He regained his number one position. He was the second man, after Lendl, who could regain a year-end number one position after losing it.

How Federer mastered the challenges and rebounded from his low points was inspirational and surely was a great demonstration of resiliency. Let us go through his roller-coaster experience more in depth. It started with Federer's first significant upset in 2008 – his semi-final straight set loss (5–7, 3–6, 6–7) to Djokovic in the Australian Open. It had been a long time since his last semi-final loss in a Grand Slam (lost to Nadal in Roland Garros in 2005), which was followed by his ten consecutive appearances in the Grand Slam finals. While the media and fans were shocked by the defeat, such a hurdle was easy for Federer to get over, as he knew what had gone wrong. He suffered from mononucleosis, a glandular fever, which cost him twenty days of practice at the beginning of the year. So the loss did not take away much of his confidence and sense of control. Expectations about Federer had piled up to almost an unreasonable level over the years. Only after release of news about his illness was the public able to digest his loss.

The aftereffect of the illness appeared to have an impact on Federer's performance over the next few months. Federer lost to several different opponents in the following Masters Series tournaments and captured only the trophy at a smaller tournament, the Estoril Open. But the next biggest shock was Nadal defeating Federer in the French Open final. The defeat itself was not at all surprising given Federer's trailing record to Nadal on the clay court and Nadal's flawless dominance in Roland Garros. What raised the alarm was the way Federer gave in his match by losing in three straight sets (1–6, 3–6, 0–6), winning only four games and swallowing a bagel, i.e. scoring zero game in a set. Despite that he was still the second best clay court player by getting into the final, significant doubt was cast on whether or not Federer was ever able to win a French Open major.

In the post-final conference, Federer firmly said yes to the question. He looked forward to the next year's French Open and said, 'I still believe that with the right mindset, with the hard work I'm going to be able to put in, hopefully…is going to help me again for next year to be even better than this year. It doesn't always need to be a victory to go out in a positive mindset.' This line of thought from Federer reflected his psychological strength. To get over the tough loss in Roland Garros, Federer tuned his mind by calling it the closure of clay court season and looking forward to get out on a grass court – his favourite surface. A forward-looking mindset helped Federer move forward rather than stand still ruminating or regretting.

When Federer was interviewed before Wimbledon, he was able to give more thoughtful reflections on how he had learnt to handle defeats more positively over the years. 'I was disappointed when I lost in earlier days. I used to cry a lot. I don't know if you remember me, but I was sort of a sad person, a very upset person…And then I used to see other players who would get so, so disappointed or upset. Sometimes they wouldn't speak for a week after. I was like, that's not the way to do it. This is supposed to be fun, and this is a dream come true for every player to play on the tour and be challenging the best in the world. So I started to relax a little bit, and I said, 'As long as I give everything on the court, that's all I can do.' And once the match is over, a different life sort of starts. This is how I see it now, and it's much better on my mind, absolutely.'

Federer's positive mindset helped him to stay motivated and keep the right spirit to take on challenges. He was not considered a strong favourite at that year's Wimbledon, which he had enjoyed being for years. Yet his self-belief helped him to play some good tennis, and he did not lose a set on his road to the final. On the day of having a chance to break the record of five consecutive Wimbledon titles, Federer lost to Nadal in an five-set epic final (4–6, 4–6, 7–6, 7–6, 7–9), which was later considered the best tennis match ever played. This was certainly a painful defeat for Federer. Wimbledon had been his land of glory. He fought back from two sets down to force a decider. The win was so close, yet so far.

In the post-match conference, Federer, who was obviously still in a demoralised state, tried his best to appreciate the match. 'It's nice to be part of it [a fantastic match],' he said. 'Probably later on in life I'll say that was a great match. But from my side, I thought I played well and everything. Missed too many chances obviously in the first couple of sets. But Rafa played well. I'm happy we lived up to the expectations. I'm happy the way I fought. That's all I could really do.'

Federer lost in the early rounds in the next two Masters Series tournaments in Toronto and Cincinnati. Not until he won the Olympic gold medal in tennis doubles with Wawrinka in August was he inspired again. The warm congratulatory reception at his home town clearly lifted Federer's spirit. But doubts about Federer remained because Federer had yet to claim a Grand Slam title in 2008. Therefore, Federer arrived in New York under considerable pressure of grabbing his last chance of winning a major for the year. Federer apparently had shouldered the pressure well, and he came through quite comfortably to win the last slam of the year, the US Open. He beat Andy Murray in three straight sets (6–2, 7–5, 6–2) in the final.

In Federer's post-match press conference, we can get some clues as to how one can set his mind to take on challenges. He approached the tournament with confidence. 'I'm always going to be confident. I'm a four-time defending champion, so I was always going to believe in my chances, and especially at the slams, I knew I was so close at Wimbledon that my chances were always going to be good here. So that's why I came into this tournament quite confident,' Federer said. After winning the slam, he tried to savour the win as much as possible and tuned in positively in projecting the future. 'I can definitely go into the rest of the season more relaxed now ... also looking forward with great spirits for next year ... I don't know what it takes to become, again, number one, but my focus is just trying to finish the year in style, and then next year I'll attack it again. I'll have many more opportunities, especially at the Masters Series and ... at the slams. The ones I wasn't able to win this year, I'll have again a chance next year.'

When Federer was asked later about his low points of 2008, he said, 'I've been trying to think of one, but every time I hit what might be considered a low, I won a title. The Estoril event came after Miami, where I'd lost to Andy. I suffered a really tough loss in the French final and won Halle, my next tournament. And after the disappointment of Wimbledon and the hard court season in America, I went to Beijing and won the doubles gold and now the [US] Open.'[48] Federer's confidence gains from his wins appeared to have more than compensated his confidence losses from his defeats. That's why his confidence had always been quite rock solid. Some match wins were already enough for him to rebuild confidence and live though his tough times.

The US Open title finally turned some criticisms of Federer to compliments. However, they did not last long. The title was only the first peak of Federer's roller-coaster journey, which was short and followed by disappointments about his performance in the last quarter of 2008, which included his round ribbon exit at

CRYSTAL WU

the ATP tour final. He suffered from back pain during the period. The beginning of the 2009 season was not particularly rewarding for Federer either. His heartfelt tears after his loss to Nadal in a five-set at Australian Open was heartbreaking. The match was so intense and close. It was his third consecutive loss to Nadal in slam finals. Federer, obviously disappointed, still tried to have the right attitude. 'This is, sure, one of the matches in my career where I feel like I could have or should have won. But you can't go through your whole life as a tennis player taking every victory that's out there. You've got to live with those,' Federer said in his post-match press conference.

Of course, the sports journalists did not necessary share the same opinion. When Federer saw it probably as only a normal slip, some saw it as a deep fall and became so ready to write him off the game. The story of a torn-down hero seemed more appealing at that time. A turnaround did not come along that soon. In the following tournaments, his performance still could not live up to standard, which had been set unbelievably high for years. He suffered three semi-final losses in Masters 1000 tournaments. What seemed more alarming was Federer's frustrated racket-cracking episode in Miami during a semi-final loss to Novak Djokovic. Federer had not lost his on-court composure for a very long time. I believe that nobody at that time would have expected or even imagined that Federer, in barely two months' time, would attain another climax of his tennis career.

Federer's incredible journey started with claiming the Madrid title by beating Rafael Nadal on clay. The win surely gave him some confidence, which he needed badly before the two majors in the summer. What happened a week later was like a drama. Federer's first week at Roland Garros was shaky, with a set loss each in the second and third round. In the other half of the draw, all eyes were on Nadal, the four-time French champion. The biggest upset of the year for tennis happened when Robin Soderling surprisingly knocked out Nadal in the fourth round. This half of the draw was suddenly left wide open. But the implication on the other half was even more. It was considered the biggest chance Federer ever had for winning his first French Open major. Should Federer have felt more relieved? He should have, as his biggest rival, particularly on clay, was gone. But pressure piled up enormously. It was as if Federer had to win the title or he was bad and would never have the chance again.

Federer survived some real scares on this tour. In the fourth round, he was down two sets against Tommy Haas and 3–4 down in the third set facing a break point. He played this crucial point bravely by hitting an inside-out forehand winner, which turned around the whole match and resulted in his winning. Federer was also pushed to fight hard in his five-set semi-final win against Juan Martin Del Potro. In the final match, the crowd was clearly one-sided and gave Federer massive support. The drama of a crazy fan approaching Federer and trying to put a hat on him was just a hiccup. People were watching to see Federer make history in tennis. He did. He played a nearly perfect match against Robin Soderling (6–1, 7–6, 6–4) to win his first French slam, complete his career Grand Slam, and tie Sampras's record of slams.

That was almost enough for many people to declare Federer's status as GOAT. For a few people, sharing the slam's record with Sampras was still not good enough. Federer gave them what they wanted right away by winning back-to-back titles in Wimbledon. In the presence of Sampras in the guest stand, Federer battled through a marathon five-set final match (5–7, 7–6, 7–6, 3–6, 16–14) against Roddick, won his sixth Wimbledon title, and more importantly, set a new slam record at fifteen slams. His place as

GOAT was more secure than ever. Once again, he was on top of the world. He regained his number one ranking. What Federer unfolded to us was his exceptionally resilient path in achieving greatness.

Finding composure in his phasing out of dominance

Being resilient does not mean that Federer can be able to maintain his match performance forever. He could have quit early due to the slightest signs showing that he was already off his peak. Then he would not have to be bothered in anyway by his shrinking dominance or harsh critics. But he wants to give his all to his tennis career. He wants to achieve more, and he loves the game so much that he wants to play as long as he can possibly play at the top level.

When Federer lost to Juan Martin Del Portro in the 2009 US Open final, people did not make a big fuss out of it. Given the strong rebound Federer had shown in the summer, people did not dare to make a prediction about Federer's possible slide, nor did they dare to say that he was never going to win another major. There were some doubts, though, concerning Federer's motivation after becoming a father and having achieved all he had. So what happened next? Federer played beautifully to win his sixteenth slam in the Australian Open in 2010. Simon Reed, a tennis expert who wrote a tennis blog for *Eurosport*, had been known for being a strong supporter of Andy Murray. He was one of those who wrote off Federer early in favour of Murray. After Federer's win against Murray in Australian Open final, he posted a blog titled 'Sorry, Fed: You're still the best' and sent a heartfelt apology to all of Federer's fans.

Federer then waited almost a year to lift another big title, winning at the 2010 World Tour Final in London. 'Every time people write me off, or try to write me off, I'm able to bounce back,' Federer said in a telephone interview with The Associated Press after the win.[49] It was more convincing than ever considering how Federer recovered from two disappointing quarter-final losses in the French Open and Wimbledon to end the 2010 season in supreme style by beating all the other top three players (Nadal, Murray, and Djokovic) and winning the Tour Final crown.

In early 2011, Federer's ranking dropped to number three for the first time since he became world number one in 2004. It surely was not easy to take. Bjorn Borg retired almost instantly after losing number one ranking at the early age of twenty-six because he lost his motivation and fire. Federer showed us the other way to deal with setbacks. Federer continued to prove that though he was not a dominant figure anymore, he remained a dangerous contestant for every tournament, especially the big ones. In the semi-final of the French Open in 2001, he broke red-hot Djokovic's forty-three-match winning streak by defeating him in four sets. He left his mark even though he did not win the title in the end.

At the end of 2011, his ranking dropped to number four, and he'd had almost a year without a title. He responded by winning three titles in a row in the last quarter of the season, including winning his first Paris Masters title and his record-breaking sixth title of World Tour Final. Federer proved again that he was there at the top and should be there for as long as he could hold up. 'Federer's season wasn't successful. But the way he lost, and the way he's subsequently bounced back, shows that there's still plenty of good tennis left in the aging superstar who hasn't quite made it over the hill,' Chris Chase, a sports writer, wrote in his tennis blog. Peter Bodo, who covered tennis over thirty years, was also thrilled by Federer's strong season end and wrote in his tennis blog, 'In 2011, Roger Federer proved that he's not just a great champion but also one of the most resilient players of all time.'

Reactions from the champion as to his increasingly dragging defeats were not perfect at the start. He lost his calmness at times on and off court. He admitted losing his confidence a bit after failing to go past the quarter-final in two consecutive Grand Slams in 2010. He had occasions where he became too defensive about his defeats. Some people in the field could sympathise with Federer's reactions. Some became critical about him to the extreme of challenging his sportsmanship, but Federer earned admiration for evolving later to regain his composure. He appeared to have redefined well his position in the game, from a dominant figure to a great player who has a good enough game to contend for the titles, including the majors. This relaxed his mind and helped him stay positive about his tennis career.

Sublime resurgence in his thirties

The strong season ended in 2011, with three consecutive titles being a wake-up call for fading believers of Federer. Many tennis followers became convinced again that the Swiss champion could truly contend for the majors, perhaps winning a few more. Yet very few believed he could ever be number one again, for that would demand him, in his thirties, to play at a consistently high level against fierce competition in the field with the presence of the other two great and in-form champions, Djokovic and Nadal. Some even believed that it made more sense for Federer to play less and keep his eyes only on the majors. On the contrary, Federer actually played more than usual, despite his increasing age and growing family size. He clearly had not let go his goal of regaining number one ranking. Not until he won four titles (Rottadam, Dubi, Indian Wells, and Madrid) in the first half of the 2012 season did people finally realise that Federer did indeed have a chance to regain the top spot.

The game's most prestigious tournament, Wimbledon, again played a crucial role in Federer's hunting for top spot this time, similar to the situation back in 2009. Before Wimbledon, while Federer was still behind Djokovic and Nadal in ranking points, he got as close as he could get to reclaiming the number one ranking. The scenario was somehow meant to be because the only way that Federer could possibly attain number one was to win the Wimbledon title. Fighting through the early scares of a five-set battle in the third round and a back injury woe in the fourth round, the determined Federer played majestic tennis in his semi-final win against Djokovic, the reigning world number one, as well as in his final win against home country hero, Murray, who was backed by the whole nation.

The milestone he achieved this time was once again historic. He won his seventh Wimbledon title, matching the all-time record held by Sampras. His seventeen Grand Slam titles set a new height, which should be out of reach for a considerable time, maybe ever. By regaining world number one ranking for the second time in his career, he broke Sampras's record of 286 weeks of number one ranking. It was special, as it happened after his two-and-a-half year drought of major titles. It was remarkable that he did it one month short of becoming thirty-one years old. Federer never stopped believing in his chance to achieve more. It was his strong belief that carried him to glory. Against the odds, Federer attained his new height of booking in 302 weeks at number one. Stefan Edberg said in a tribute video, "The longer he stays in tennis, the better it is for tennis.' Very true. It is good for the game to have Federer hanging around longer and happier. Anyone who really loves tennis will hope to see Federer remain on tour for as long as he can, for we all admire his sheer dignity in accomplishing his goals in his tennis career.

Development of resilience depends very much on one's earlier experiences and learning. A child growing up in an overprotective environment will likely turn into an adult who is more vulnerable in downturns. With sensible parents, Federer did have enough chances to grow tougher during his upbringing. For example, the first big challenge the young Federer faced was his move to live and train in Ecublens alone when he turned fourteen. He left his closely bonded family and lived with a host family. He had no friends there and was the youngest trainee in the tennis programme. The worst part was the language barrier. A boy who could barely speak French struggled in the French-speaking part of the country. Understandably, the young Federer felt sad and homesick for a couple of months. He cried and called home quite often. His tennis suffered as well because he had dampened motivation. His frustration manifested itself in some bad behaviours, such as more racket throwing. He was basically not happy at that time.

Federer could have given up, but he did not. His parents, of course, gave him a great deal of support. They had a strong belief in their son. They did not just pull him out of the hole and ask him to quit. They talked him into staying and facing the challenge. Federer's mad love of tennis and commitment to his goal helped him to hang in there and find his way through. He later grew more settled and accustomed to his life in Ecublens. He got along well with the hosting family and made some new friends. He gradually learnt and mastered a new language – French. He built up his strengths and psychological resources during this tough period. Such experience clearly had much positive impact on the young Federer and his later development.

Federer's mother's comment in an interview best summed up what the experience meant to Federer. She said, 'It was a great lesson in life for him – that things don't always go your own way, and that you don't get anywhere in life with talent alone. You have to work at things. I know it wasn't always fun and games for Roger there, and that many days he wasn't that happy, but those struggles were good for him. Overcoming those ups and downs was a challenge for him, and it helped him to develop as a person.'[50]

Perhaps one of the biggest life challenges for anyone is to face the death of a beloved one, despite that we all know about the inevitability of death. It is so hard to take that some people may feel as if they've dropped into a deep hole that may require years to come out of. The grieving process takes on different phrases. A person who loses a significant one may first find the news of death too shocking to digest, coupled with a sense of disbelief and numbness. There may be a denial phase, with the person crying out 'I can't believe it' or 'It isn't true'. After accepting the reality of loss, the person needs to work through the pain of grief. This is the stage when the person actually feels the pain – whether sadness, anger, or guilt – and expresses the grief. How long this stage takes varies a great deal. Intrapersonal conflicts and complications in this stage are somewhat common. When people can finally make sense and meaning out of the tragedy, they can learn to cope with the loss and then move on with their lives.

The death of Peter Carter, Federer's first coach, in 2002 definitely came as a big shock to Federer. He was playing the tennis Masters Series in Toronto around the time. The news came the night right after he lost his first single round. He was alone, still frustrated with his loss, when he heard the shocking news about the sudden death of Carter in a car accident in South Africa. He felt so terrible that night for losing his mentor. He was filled with guilt, as he was the one who suggested Carter take a safari trip in South Africa. He bore the pain and grief. He went on to lose the double in Toronto and lost again in the first round in Cincinnati.

Fortunately, Federer was not shy about expressing his grief to his family and friends. He took part in the funeral, which somewhat facilitated his grieving. 'I usually try to avoid sad events like this,' he said some weeks after the funeral. 'It was the first time that I'd been to a funeral. I can't say that it did me good, but I was close to him in thought once again and I could say goodbye in a dignified setting. I feel a bit better, especially in terms of tennis. The motivation that I felt I'd lost after the event is back.'

Federer emerged stronger, as he could now take defeats more easily. He realised that any defeat in tennis could hardly compare with some other bigger losses in life. He also learnt to see the positive things in defeat. Federer's later success in tennis provided Peter Carter's parents a bit of consolation. On TV in a town in Australia, Carter's parents watched the match in which Federer won his first slam. It happened less than a year after Peter's death. They shed tears. Bob Carter explained their feelings towards Federer's win. 'It's a wonderful feeling, really, because Peter had such an influence on his career, and to watch Roger play, you can sort of see a little of Peter there.'[14] It probably helped ease the pain of their loss.

In the semi-final between Switzerland and Australia for the Davis Cup, the Peter Carter Memorial Trophy was first introduced to award to the winning team in memorial of Peter Carter. You can imagine how desperately Federer wanted to win the trophy, named after his respected coach. Federer won his first match, but the Swiss team was then down 2–1. Federer had to beat Hewitt to keep the tie alive. A tense five-set match ended with Federer's loss, and he ran off the court sobbing. The two teams met Carter's parents later in a dressing room. At this first meeting with Peter's parents since Peter died, Federer broke down again. Peter's parents consoled and comforted Federer. Federer said, 'It was hard to lose, and [Peter's] parents came in and I got more emotional – so many emotions. But it was important for me to face it.'

Some people might forget or not even be aware that Federer was once considered a super-talented tennis player failing at finding his place in slams. Between 2001 and the middle of 2003, Federer never got past the quarters of Grand Slam tournaments, with several opening-round losses. That was his dark period in terms of slams results. Some tennis pundits even doubted he would ever win a slam. Of course, among so many players, only a few could eventually win a slam. However, Federer's stunning performance and achievements in smaller tournaments piled much expectation on him and thus made his slumps in slams major setbacks in his tennis career during that time.

In 2003, with his faith and commitment in the game, he again declared his ambition to win a slam. The start was not good, as he lost to David Nalbandian in round sixteen in the Australian Open. An even more shocking loss awaited him in the next slam, the French Open. He lost to an unknown opponent in the first round. The loss cruelly labelled Federer somewhat as a Grand Slam loser. He later admitted that he failed mentally in the match. He was unable to shoulder the pressure and felt he was losing control. No one at that point could have thought that this brutal defeat would immediately be followed by Federer's dawning period of an unbelievable run at slams.

Federer was so talented that he had too many options on the court. He needed to work on figuring out how he could choose right options at right moments. He needed to assemble and put together all his components in place to achieve greater success. This represented a big challenge for him. Federer managed to arrive at Wimbledon with a refreshed mindset in 2003. Carrying on his success at a pre-Wimbledon grass court tournament in Halle, he regained his sense of control with an optimistic mind. He believed he had his chance on a grass court. His faith and his game led him through to his first Grand Slam final. On his way, he battled not only against tough opponents like Andy Roddick but also against his own back pain, which suddenly emerged in the middle of the tournament. A dream-come-true moment for Federer happened when his final opponent, Mark Philippoussis, failed to return his serve at the championship point. Federer finally won his first Grand Slam, breaking through the Grand Slam blockage and entering his dominant years in slams.

Adversities are inevitable in life. Fortunately, we can learn resilience. Every time we live though adversities or overcome life hurdles, we accumulate invaluable experiences and memories for us to call upon when we face new challenges. To enhance our resilience, we need to adopt the right attitudes and strengthen some other associated qualities. The following are some examples:

- Commit to goals and plans. Do not pull out easily due to setbacks. Be ready to devote enough time and effort to overcome obstacles.

- Believe that we have the ability to exert control over our life experiences and that our input matters and can affect the outcome.

- Reframe adversity or setback as a challenge and opportunity for personal growth.

- Do not avoid dealing with adversities. Remember, avoidance deprives us of learning opportunities.

- Build up our character strengths with hope and optimism.

- Enhance our self-esteem. Self-worth is an important protective factor in our downturn. We may engage ourselves in activities or tasks that we are good at and derive satisfaction and self-affirmation as much as possible from them.

- Be able to recognise and regulate our emotions. Negative emotions significantly narrow our minds and behavioural repertoire, thus limiting our ability to overcome obstacles. Better mood management fosters resilience.

- Build social resources. We need both concrete help and emotional support from our friends, particularly in tough times. We also have to learn to use our social resources effectively and reach out to the right person for advice.

- Control our impulses. Resilient people do not jump to conclusions or decisions. We should learn to sit back and think thoroughly before acting.

- Enhance our problem-solving skills. Try to work out solutions for our life problems.

Afterword
and
Acknowledgements

This book is written based on the assumption that people normally do care about their well-being and want to have a flourished life. If you do, I hope you enjoyed reading this book and are able to get some ideas about how you are going to enhance your own well-being. Assuming you are a lover of sports too, this book may have shown you the ways to enjoy your sports even more. Forgive me if you are not at all familiar with tennis or Federer. I hope my enthusiasm was not too much for you.

While I am a loyal fan of Roger Federer, I am not the kind of fan who dislikes and picks on idol's competitors for the sake of showing loyalty. Loving Federer has not ruled out my appreciation for other players. I like Nadal's on-court fighting spirit and his sportsmanship. Nadal is as nice and humble as Federer and is cute with his shy personality. I also greatly appreciate his genuine respect for Federer. Roddick and Djokovic both have a good sense of humour, even though their jokes can sometimes be a bit offensive to others. Many other players in the tennis field also play fairly, work hard, and have decent personalities. During the period I was writing this book, Michael Phelps, the best swimming champion at the time, was accused of marijuana use. It was disappointing and made me even more appreciative of having such a good role model - Roger Federer. Federer succeeded in his young age with so much dominance. Yet he did not get himself lost in a hole or high in the sky. He handled his success very well. He remains honest, humble, and respectful to others. He has always lived a healthy and pleasant life.

I do not want to sound as if there is no negative at all about Federer and that Federer is simply flawless. 'Flawless' is just a nice adjective that we use to express our deep appreciation. Like when Federer played at his best, many people said he had a flawless game. Did it mean that he played perfectly at every point? No. He still had unforced errors, double faults, and bad shot selections at some points during a match. It was the way he played the match that left us with an unbelievably great impression. It's the same when we look into one's personality and life; we consider a bigger picture rather than focusing on flaws. Federer has bad days too. He still throws his racket, though rarely now. He was fined for using profanity at the US Open 2009 final. He was accused of using injuries as excuses after some of his big losses. Federer can suffer slips in confidence and mental toughness sometimes. Occasionally, he gets annoyed and gives short and blunt answers to repeatedly asked negative questions.

I just want to tell you that negative emotions, behaviours, and thoughts are just part of human nature. We do not necessarily need to reject them. Greater acceptance towards the negatives is as important as greater appreciation towards the positives. Role model does not demand perfectionism. It is not a prototype for us to copy or follow. It just brings us inspiration and adds more life perspectives. Some people might argue, 'If I had the Roger's talent, I would have the great life he did.' Yes, maybe. This is not an unusual argument. But from my clinical experience, one can be very talented and still live a miserable life. On the other hand, one does not need to be gifted to live a happy and satisfied life.

Finally, I would like to thank Roger Federer for the inspirations he has brought to me and for all the joy I have watching him play and following his career. Following Federer's tennis and stories has brought me much fun and excitement. My husband and I were attracted to tennis because of him. Tennis then became an important shared hobby in my family and has been integrated into our everyday lives – like spending time playing, watching, and talking about tennis. I also have developed a ritual of treating my colleagues to a round of snacks whenever Federer wins significant tournaments. This started with a promise I made, when Federer had not won a title for a while in 2008, that I would give colleagues a treat if Federer won a title. He did it at the Madrid Masters tournament, and I delivered my promise. Since then, I could not stop the ritual, as my colleagues intentionally induced a superstitious idea that if I stopped treating them, Federer would not win another title. I am not at all superstitious. I think I continued the practice because it became a valuable savouring experience for me to celebrate Federer's every win. I guess I will never get a chance to send Federer a bill for the charges. But I hope I will have a chance to give back for the joy and enlightenment Federer has brought to me. I hope this book can serve that purpose a bit. I am sending all my best wishes to Roger Federer, his family, and his tennis.

Finally, I would like to thank my dearest husband, Hyman, for sharing my passion for tennis and encouraging me about writing this book. I would also like to thank my parents and sister for supporting me in pursuing my career and interests all the way. I am greatly appreciative for the excitement shown by my good friends, including Sally, Michelle and Carmen, when I shared with them my publication idea. Finally, I am thankful for my colleagues, who have positively reinforced my love for tennis.

ABOUT THE AUTHOR

The author, Crystal Wu, is a clinical psychologist and a positive psychologist. Her day-to-day job is providing psychotherapy for her clients, helping them to recover from their sufferings and achieve better well-being. She has faith in positive psychological strengths in people and believes happiness and flourishing are ultimate pursuits of life. Also a sports enthusiast, Crystal is a fan of many sports and is active in playing sports herself, especially tennis and Chinese martial arts. She is convinced that sports are beneficial to health and are life enriching.

References

(1) Seligman, Martin E.P. *Authentic Happiness: Using the New Positive Psychology to Realise Your Potential for Lasting Fulfillment*, New York: Free Press, 2002.

(2) Seligman, Martin E.P. *Flourish: A Visionary New Understanding of Happiness and Well-Being*, New York: Free Press, 2011.

(3) Farrow, Paul E. Federer Is First Rate, *Tennis Week*, 2006.

(4) Kimmage, Paul. Roger Federer: Confessions of a Tennis Dad, *Sunday Times*, 2009.

(5) Biswas, Dipanntia Ghosh. I'm an Extremely Balanced Person, *Times of India*, 2006.

(6) Gimelstob, Justin. Getting to Know Roger off the Court: the World No. 1 Is Weirdly Down to Earth, *Sports Illustrated*, 2008.

(7) Sarkar, Pritha. Interview – Reuters Q&A with Grand Slam King Federer, Reuters, 2009.

(8) Granderson, LZ. Tragic Deaths Taught Federer and Sampras to Live for the Moment, *ESPN*, 2008.

(9) Harman, Neil. The Net Post: Roger Federer's Resurgence Breathes New Life into Tennis, *Times*, 2009.

(10) Nakamura, J. and Csikszentmihalyi, M. *Flow Theory and Research*, 2001, in C. R. Snyder, Erik Wright, and Shane J. Lopez, *Handbook of Positive Psychology*, Oxford University Press, pp. 195–206, 2005.

(11) Csikszentmihalyi, M. and Abuhamdeh, M. *Flow*, 2005, in Elliot, A., *Handbook of Competence and Motivation*, New York: The Guilford Press, pp. 598–698, 2007.

(12) Ford, Bonnie D. Motivation is bigger than ever for Roger Federer, *ESPN*, 2007.

(13) Le Grand, Chip. Federer in the Court of Kings, *The Australian*, 2005.

(14) Bowers, Chris. *Roger Federer: Spirit of a Champion*, John Blake, 2009.

(15) Stauffer, Rene. *The Roger Federer Story: Quest For Perfection*, New Chapter Press, 2007.

(16) Mathabane, Mark. Roger Federer: The Making of a Global Ambassador, *Deuce*, 2005.

(17) Dickson, Mike. Roger Federer's Smooth Approach Makes Him the Best His Game Can Get, *Daily Mail*, 2010.

(18) Agassi, Andre. *Open: An Autobiography*, Knopf Doubleday Publishing Group, 2010.

(19) Folley, Malcolm. The Woman Behind the Modern-Day Borg', *Daily Mail*, 2007.

(20) Tebbutt, Tom. Federer, Nadal Give Game Quite the 1-2 Punch', *The Globe and Mail*, 2007.

(21) Fest, Sebastian. Federer Sees Himself "Very Far" from Best Player in History, DPA, 2007.

(22) Roberts, Selena. It's Time to Welcome a Symbol of Substance, *New York Times*, 2007.

(23) Pinto, Pedro. Federer Tells CNN – I'm Still Motivated, CNN, 2009. http://edition.cnn.com/2009/SPORT/11/17/ tennis.federer.interview/index.html

(24) Halloran, Jessica. Roche Finds Time for Mr Nice Guy, *Sydney Morning Herald*, 2006.

(25) Hodgkinson, Mark. Pete Sampras: Federer Can Take My Records, *Telegraph*, 2007.

(26) Pitt, Nick. The Big Interview: Roger Federer, *Sunday Times*, 2004.

(27) Roberts, John. Federer Takes the Plaudits in Role As Natural Champion, *Independent*, 2004.

(28) Araton, Harvey. Open Emotions from Federer, *New York Times*, 2009.

(29) Norrish, Mike. French Open 2009: Roger Federer Deserves to Make History, says Tim Henman, *Telegraph*, 2009.

(30) Harman, Neil. Federer a Player in Charge of His Destiny, *Times*, 2010.

(31) Falbo, Marco. What We Can Learn from Roger Federer, Credit Suisse, 2013.

(32) Simons, Bill. Thus Spoke: Roger Federer, *Inside Tennis*, 2008.

(33) Rossingh, Danielle. and Bandel, Carolyn. Federer's Success Gets Swiss Talking of William Tell, Not Banks, Bloomberg, 2009.

(34) Laver, Rod. Time 100 – Heroes & Pioneers – Roger Federer, *Time*, 2007.

(35) Hodgkinson, Mark. Pete Sampras: Federer Can Take My Records', *Telegraph*, 2007.

(36) Boeck, Greg. Low-Key Federer on Top of World, *USA Today*, 2004.

(37) Khlongtoey, Krissie. Love of the game, *Bangkok Post*, 2004.

(38) Alvanipour, Sarah. Big Hit: High-Schooler Gets to Practice with Federer, *TENNIS*, 2007.

(39) Clarey, Christopher. Federer the Conqueror Isn't Done Yet, *New York Times*, 2005.

(40) Pearce, Linda. Perfect Federer Admits to Hard Days on Court, *The Age*, 2006.

(41) Jimenez, Tony. Federer Plans to Dominate for Another Five Years at Least, Reuters, 2007.

(42) Swanton, Will. Roger the Record-Slayer, *Sydney Morning Herald*, 2008.

(43) Harrell, Eben. Greatest Hitter: Roger Federer, *Time*, 2009.

(44) Preston, Eleanor. Champion Is Reaping Rich Rewards from 10 Years of Toil, *Guardian*, 2005.

(45) Federer Backs Bans for Tennis Gamblers, AFP, http://www.theage.com.au/news/tennis/federer-backs-bans-for-tennis-gamblers/2007/11/11/1194329578073.html

(46) Sengupta, Jaydip. Federer: I Don't Work on Weaknesses', Xpress, 2009.

(47) Ford, Bonnie D. Fed not ready for rubber chicken circuit, *ESPN*, 2010.

(48) Harman, Neil. Roger Federer's Resurgence Breathes New Life into Tennis, *Times*, 2008.

(49) Fendrich, Howard. Federer Proud of Bouncing Back to Close 2010 Well after Inconsistent Performance All Year, *Lubbock Avalanche-Journal*, 2010.

(50) Hodgkinson, Mark. The Making of a Champion, *Telegraph*, 2005.